The American Indian Medicine Dreambook

Brad Steiger

77 Lower Valley Road
Atglen, PA 19310

Cover Artwork by S.W. Ferguson

Library of Congress Catalog Number:
93-060016

ISBN:0-924608-14-5

Published by Whitford Press
A Division of Schiffer Publishing, Ltd.
77 Lower Valley Road
Atglen, Pennsylvania 19310
Please write for a free catalog.
This book may be purchased from the publisher.
Please include $2.95 for shipping and handling.
Try your bookstore first.

We are always interested in hearing from authors
with book ideas on related subjects.

Contents

Contents

Follow the Medicine Path

To follow the Medicine path was deemed to be one of the highest callings that a traditional Indian could pursue in the structured world of tribal life. Most tribes believed that those endowed with true shamanistic gifts were born with them and that the sure signs of that sacred calling would be exhibited almost as soon as the special children were able to speak.

Indian lore is filled with stories of young men and women who were touched by the Great Mystery early in their lives and were given the marvelous gift of healing.

Often children with that special blessing would climb into the laps of those suffering from, let us say, a headache and place their lips against the forehead of the one in anguish. The children would inhale a breath, then turn away and exhale it, repeating the movements in a ritualistic manner until the "evil spirit" had been sucked from the throbbing cranium.

Those to whom the secrets of healing were revealed would enter a world in which great honor awaited, but one in which duty and responsibility also dominated.

Those men and women who became the greatest of shamans were expected to live especially noble lives and to demonstrate restraint in the face of travail that was not demanded of tribal members of lesser standing.

One of the earliest representations of a
shaman, a Medicine Priest, is over 15,000 years
old and was found in a Stone Age cave in what is
now southwestern France.

The curative practices of the Medicine people of this continent are often viewed today as a skillful blend of herbal pharmacology and the practical application of psychological principles that the white doctors did not learn until the advent of modern psychotherapy. The restoratives given to patients came always from the familiar plants of the earth, for as the shaman knew, life came from the Earth Mother and with the fruits of her abundance came health.

For countless generations, those who followed the Medicine path experimented with the herbs and roots of their native environment until they knew intimately the effects that each had on different parts of the human body and the extent of their beneficial properties in combating different types of illnesses.

As the modern science of pharmacology advances, increasing numbers of the curative plants used in shamanic healing techniques are being found to be effective for nearly all of the same purposes that the ancient tribal doctors had used them. These tested nostrums have found their way back into the magic black bags of our contemporary physicians.

The psychology of the Mind-Body-Spirit link-up that must be employed in order to heal the whole person was developed by Medicine priests hundreds of years before the earliest realization of white culture that the mind is the greatest contributor to the restoration of a patient's health. A great number of today's most effective wholistic healing practitioners are aware of the great debt that they owe to the Native American Medicine people of the past.

To the Indian, all cures came through the agency of the Great Mystery. When the shaman entered the hogan of one who lay ill, the patient as well as the Medicine priest knew that it was the Great Mystery who was coming to bring healing. The infirm would feel better just knowing that a beneficent Force had entered his home in the visible form of the Medicine priest.

The shaman would bring with him magical healing artifacts which patients had learned from childhood to revere. They had seen the sacred objects aid others in their curative powers, and they had confidence that the magic of their energy would also help them to recover from their ailments.

In the shaman's medicine bag were several items that produced a calming effect on the patients because of their recognized magical and mystical potency. Depending on the tribe, one might find within the medicine bag a number of stones, which very often included turquoise and crystal; bird feathers, such as the sacred eagle's; a small, symbolic clay image of an aspect of the Great Mystery; and certain medicinal herbs.

The drum and the rattle which so many Medicine priests carried served two very good purposes in the practice of healing. They gave rhythm to the sacred medicine chants, and they were useful in distracting the patients from their pain and allowing them to focus on the efforts of the shaman to make them well.

In the regulated structure of most tribes, the Medicine priests were the ones who healed hearts, as well as bodies; and they served as the first marriage counselors in North America. Suitors who had quarreled with their intended, or husbands and wives who had taken to throwing grindstones at each other, sought out the Medicine priests and abided by their sage counsel when they had presented both sides of the spat before them.

The Medicine practitioners gave the hostile parties commonsense advice based on the wisdom accumulated as the tribe's spiritual leaders, and their words usually had the power to patch domestic strife in a fashion that left both husband and wife with their dignity intact and a workable solution at hand.

In their revered positions as spiritual leaders, the Medicine priests had also to be prepared to assume the role similar to that of a father confessor. For example, if an errant member of the tribe had stolen something from another and was suffering pangs of conscience, he would call upon the respected tribal counselor and seek a way to undo the harm that he had committed by his theft.

In such an instance, the Medicine priest might take the stolen object and see that it was returned to the rightful owner, without the identity of the thief being made known to his victim. But the wrongdoer who had violated the strict tribal laws against theft would find that he had been given a stiff penance by the Medicine priest. He may have to perform a long list of good deeds around the village within a certain period of time--and he knew that the shaman kept a careful watch to be certain that all the tasks were completed on schedule.

Pictoglyph of a Medicine Priest's lodge.

In such a manner, the Medicine priest not only healed the bodies of the tribe, but he also helped to cure the social ills that could threaten the total well being of the village.

Perhaps even more important than the role of healer of physical bodies and societal ills was the Medicine priest's function as spiritual arbiter between the worlds of life and death, the dimensions of flesh and spirit. Nearly all the tribes relied almost totally upon their

Medicine priests to perform the spiritual rites and rituals that would assure them safe passage from one life to
the next.

The ancient medicine dances called down special
blessings on war or hunting parties before they set off
from the village, but the most sacred of dances held
open the entrance to the spirit world so the soul of the
recently departed could safely join the grandparents in
the new life within the very heart of the Great Mystery.

As the shamanic priests instructed their tribes in the
way of life that would best insure their acceptance in
the world of spirit, they emphasized eight essential
elements in Medicine power:

1. The vision quest, with its emphasis on self-denial and spiritual
discipline, extended to a life-long pursuit of wisdom of body and soul.

2. A reliance upon one's personal visions and dreams to provide
one's direction on the path of life.

3. A search for personal songs to enable one to attune oneself to
the primal sound, the cosmic vibration of the Great Mystery.

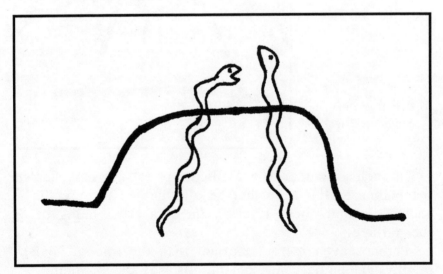

In this pictoglyph we see the line of the sky and two serpents peering
above it, thus denoting how they receive their knowledge of divine things.
Medicine Priests, properly disciplined, could speak the language of
serpents and learn sacred secrets directly from them.

4. A belief in the total partnership with the world of spirits and the ability to make personal contact with grandfathers and grandmothers who have changed planes of existence.

5. The possession of a non-linear time sense.

6. A receptivity to the evidence that the essence of the Great Mystery may be found in everything.

A reverence and a passion for the Earth Mother, the awareness of one's place in the web of life and of one's responsibility toward all plant and animal life.

8. A total commitment to one's belief that pervades ever aspect of one's life and enables one truly to walk in balance.

In October of 1974, Grandmother Twylah of the Seneca received a great revelation about the Medicine people. Their paths have crossed before, she said, because the primary urge of those who seek Medicine Power is to be of service to all humankind.

"Medicine people have always been together, evolving through many former lives along the same level of development, being guided by the teachers of spiritual wisdom," Twylah said. "Medicine people cling as one because of our devotion to the Creator.

"We have learned who we are...where we came from...why we are here...and what the future has in store for us. We have learned that we are of the Great Light....We are presently here because we are aware of the coming cleansing of Mother Earth, our caretaker."

After the Great Purification of the Mother has taken place with all the attendant earth changes, vulcanisms, and cataclysms, Twylah said that the Medicine people will carry on and seed the decrees of the Creator into the next world after the cleansing.

"During this time," she continued, "some Medicine people will evolve as people of wisdom...some will be teachers...some will be messengers. Each messenger will assist others in seeking the Pathway of Peace according to the level of his gifts and abilities.

"Medicine people are recognized by other Medicine people, and they know that they are on their earthwalk to heal and to help others.

"Our future and the future of all beings lies in the survival of the perfection of the Creator. Medicine people
know that there is only one universal Source, and everyone
is equal within the Source. Our unity is secure and complete, as we join all Medicine people, people of wisdom,
and seekers of the truth.

Na-na-bush, the intercessor, is a figure that ex-
presses the legend held by some tribes that at one time
an aspect of the Creator assumed human form and
taught the people many valuable crafts and arts. This
facet of the Great Mystery may be reached by a
Medicine Priest through spirit contact.

"It is the duty of Medicine people to share their spiritual growth. Spiritual development can only be measured by the sincere dialogue carried on around the Council fire. No one dominates at the council because of the Medicine belief of equality. Patience is a virtue characteristic of Medicine people. Each member of the lodge takes a turn to share thoughts, impressions, feelings, communications, and wisdom. Medicine people communicate spiritually in order to nurture our seeds of development--and when they are ripe, we blossom forth in a burst of wisdom.

"In thanksgiving," Grandmother Twylah concluded, "we Medicine people place ourselves and all our affairs into spiritual hands, thus feeling secure. We vow never to lose the grasp of the great gift of Medicine Power."

Entering Dreamtime

I learned how to control my dreams quite by accident. I was only a boy of eight or nine and suffering from horrible nightmares. One night, in the throes of a terrible dream in which I was surrounded by an ever-closing circle of monsters, it suddenly occurred to me to step outside of my dream.

When I demanded to know just *whose* dream it was, the monsters ceased their threatening movements and meekly conceded that it was my dream. As if I were the director of a motion picture, I proceded to instruct the hideous actors that they would henceforth fall dead or disappear at my signal-- and without hesitation or argument. Once again the previously fearsome monsters proved to be quite decent fellows, and they agreed to obey my every wish. It was, after all, *my* dream. To console the monsters, I reminded them that they would not really die, since it was all make-believe anyway.

It has now been nearly fifty years since that fateful night when I assumed control over my dreams, and I have never experienced another nightmare. As a student, I used my dreams to review material before a classroom test, to memorize my catechism lessons for the pastor, to prepare myself for oral examinations by rehearsing the material over and over again in dreamtime. As a young adult, I planned the day ahead, "wrote" the first drafts of my books and articles, and, on occasion, re-

leased stress and tension by devising dream scenarios
that would make John Wayne or Chuck Norris look
like choirboys tussling between church services.

It was not until I was thirty-one that my first true
mentor, a wise elder from the Winnebago tradition,
made me aware that one could enter dreamtime to communicate with other levels of reality, to receive teaching visions, to travel in the spirit body to other dimensions, and to heal oneself and others. Today, as I approach sixty years of age, I have been privileged to
have learned many additional methods of becoming a
"dream catcher" from great teachers from the traditions
of the Chippewa, the Seneca, the Mesquakie, the Teton
Sioux, the Hopi, the Navajo, the Cherokee, the Cree,
and many others. It is now time for me to share, as did
my first mentor, the symbols, signs, and methods employed in the productive utilization of dreamtime.

Central to the core belief of all Medicine practitioners is a reliance on one's personal visions and dreams to
provide one's direction on the path of life. By learning
how to interpret your own dream symbols according to
the ancient wisdom of Medicine Priests, you can become
a "Dream Catcher" and begin at once to create a better
life in the here and now--and in your future.

Shamans have known for hundreds of years that the
Soul, the Spirit, the Essential Self within each human
being has the ability to rise to a level of consciousness
wherein past, present, and future blend together to form
an Eternal Now. It is in this dimension of spirit that
you will receive important teachings, guidance, and
prophecies relevant to your life and to the lives of your
friends and loved ones.

The power of Dreamtime has been known to all
Medicine Priests for centuries, and it is an essential
aspect of the wisdom of the shaman to be able to travel
in this dimension free of time and space. The Medicine
Priests know that it is within one's dreams that visions
live an independent existence of their own, patiently
awaiting the opportunity to reveal their wisdom to the
true seeker.

A Dream Catcher

Some Medicine practitioners make a Dream Catcher to serve as a physical stimulus to "Catching," that is, remembering their dreams. The thongs that bind the net to the outer rim should be very thin, simulating spider webs. Any symbol that appeals to the dreamer, such as a totem animal, may be painted upon the shield within the net.

In the solitary, mystical experience of entering Dreamtime, we can enter a dimension of reality between the physical and the nonphysical, the world of spirits and the world of humans, the state of being and the state of nothingness. Here, in this in-between world, we can discover the solutions to our deepest distresses and our most forlorn yearnings. We can free ourselves of the demands of clockwork time and find ourselves liberated to travel in our spirit bodies to an eternity beyond the measure of hours and years and beyond the deep silence of the stars.

"When I was a boy," Silver Cloud, my Winnebago teacher said, "I would get up in the morning, get something to eat, and maybe work for many hours before I really woke up. And then I would sit there bewildered, not really knowing where I was. My parents were worried about me, because I did this a lot.

"One day the Medicine Priest observed me 'wake up' after we had been picking berries for several hours. He told me not worry, that I was one of those people whose spirit visited the Summerland [a peaceful spiritual dimension] while my physical body slept. Sometimes, he told me, the spirit did not get properly connected with the brain before the body awoke."

The Medicine Priest told Silver Cloud that long ago in dawn time the people were so closely in harmony with the Creator that they did most of their talking with their mind, instead of the mouth. But as the people became more and more interested in the physical things that they deemed important, they moved farther away from attunement with the Creator Spirit and they spent more time worrying about the body than about the spirit. In dreamtime, however, one could still travel to Summerland and other places in the spirit body.

"The Medicine Priest stressed that we humans needed both the physical and the spiritual to achieve balance in our lives," Silver Cloud said. "We could not spend all of our time in contemplation and meditation--or in dreaming. We were given both a body and a spirit by the Great Mystery, and we are expected to use both in a positive and constructive way."

Silver Cloud and other great Medicine teachers have stated that the part of our mind that creates dreams may be controlled by our guide and utilized to convey bits of truths and teachings that we need to learn. The dream may also be used by our guide to prepare us for the unpleasant aspects of life on the earthplane.

"You, the individual, are the one best qualified to interpret your dreams," Silver Cloud stated often and firmly. "It is good to study symbols and the history of things to help you understand the deeper meaning of your dreams. The more you understand about your culture and its history, the more you can understand the language in which the deeper, older levels of your mind speak to you."

For the Medicine Priest, time in its linear sense, as most of us understand it best, does not really exist. For the higher levels of spirit consciousness, time is an Eternal Now. It is only on the earth plane, where things must occur in sequence, that linear time exists. When we sleep, however, and enter Dreamtime, we have also entered a timeless realm.

"In our dreams there is an awareness that life is continuous," Silver Cloud said, "whether on Earth or in the spheres beyond Earth."

But how does one bring mental awareness into a dream in order to catch the symbols without shattering the reality of Dreamtime?

Although we can simulate the dream process through hypnosis and other altered states techniques, we are not truly entering Dreamtime if we are guided through its ethereal arches by someone leading us through the steps of a process. What we can achieve by an altered state techniques is a "priming of the pump," so to speak. We can put ourselves into a mental set, a state of deep relaxation, which, thereby, prepares us to dream.

As I stated earlier, I discovered quite by accident--or

necessity, if you prefer--that I could step outside of my frightening dream and assume command of its action. Once I had accomplished this feat, I had the awareness that I could do it again. Unconsciously, then, I programmed myself with the realization that whenever a

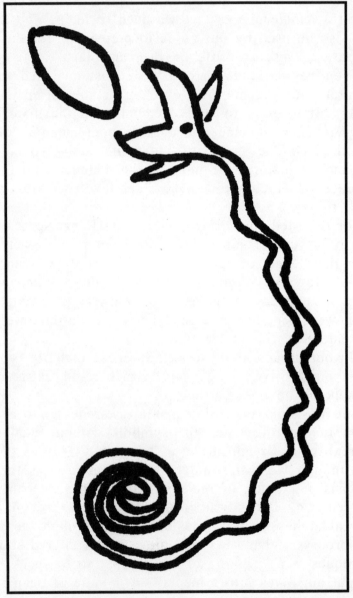

Representation of the Great Serpent Mound of Ohio in pictoglyph. Some believe the symbol portrays the creative energy of the sun.

dream scenario takes a turn that becomes too frightening, too threatening, or too unpleasant, I have the ability to stop the action, and, like any experienced and assertive director, take control of the drama and redirect the flow not only to my liking, but to my good and gaining.

It is always difficult to teach others a method or technique that has become second nature to oneself. If, let us say, I should wish to dream of spending the day in an Indian village as it might have existed in the last century, I lie quietly before falling asleep, reviewing in my brain everything that I know intellectually about Amerindian life during that period of linear time. Next, I "rehearse" my dreamwalk. I begin a number of scenarios that I could enjoy experiencing during my dream. I also repeat again and again the affirmation that I know that I have the ability to accomplish such a goal--and I remind my higher levels of consciousness that I have done so many, many times on previous occasions. Soon, I begin to hear snatches of conversation, perhaps the sound of a flute, the beat of drum, the laughter of children--and I am in the midst of my dream, which continues of its own volition until I awake. I should quickly amend that it continues of its own volition unless some action occurs which I chose to alter and redirect.

In comparing notes with Medicine teachers over the years, I have found that they employ similar techniques. Once Sun Bear, the great Chippewa Medicine Priest, remembered how he had learned from an uncle how to "dream" where the best deer hunting would be found. Basically, one focused on the deer group spirit, reviewed a number of likely hunting areas, then fell asleep and dreamed of the precise spot where the next day's hunt would be successful.

Silver Cloud recalled the time when he, as a boy, fell asleep and dreamed where the herd of cattle had strayed. Not only did he locate the exact area of the forest where they grazed, but he focused in on a cow in labor giving birth to a calf that needed help desperately. "I awakened and went right to the place where the herd had strayed, and I was able to help the cow give a more uncomplicated birth," he said.

If you are having difficulty entering Dreamtime, I offer here a technique that should prove to be of great assistance. You may read the following two or three times before you fall asleep at night. If you are not successful on the first evening, you should not be at all discouraged. Anything worthwhile takes time, and things of the spirit cannot be legislated by the demands of our instant "plop-plop, fizz-fizz" society. Spiritual development requires time and a great deal of self-discipline.

If you prefer, you may try recording the programming on a cassette tape. If you do this, I recommend that you record three minutes of soft, restful classical, New Age, or traditional Indian flute music before you repeat the following words in your own voice:

> "I have been sincerely working on my spiritual development and on entering Dreamtime. I know that I have the ability to achieve control of my dreams, but at the present time I require assistance from my guide.
>
> "I know that I have the ability to receive symbols from my dreams that will give me great assistance in my life, but at the present time, I need my guide to provide me with the key to the door to Dreamtime.
>
> "I know that I have the ability to accomplish all of these things. I know that I can achieve higher levels of awareness.
>
> "I know that when I awake, I will remember the key to Dreamtime that my guide has given me."

You should speak these words in a slow, measured, confident voice. When you have completed reading the above, record another three minutes and repeat the verbal programming. If you wish, you may replicate the process a third, fourth, or fifth time--as often as your tape will allow. Place the cassette player beside your bed or use a speaker under your pillow and allow it to play the tape through until you fall asleep. Repeat this process until you have achieved the desired results.

Identifying Your
Totem Animal
and Spirit Guide

Silver Cloud and perhaps most traditional Indians would admonish us that one cannot truly enter Dreamtime and properly receive its teachings until one has learned the identity of the totem animal and/or the spirit guide.

Among traditional Indians the totem is a symbol of the name of the sacred progenitor-—some member of the animal kingdom--which stands as the surname of the family. Ancient legends tell of the Great Mystery transforming certain members of the bear family, the deer family, the wolf family, the turtle family, and so on, into two-legged humans, thus shaping the genesis of the various clans. In the old days, individuals unhesitatingly traced their lineage from a four-legged creature, bird, or reptile. By whatever other names the traditional Indians might be called in their lifetimes, it was the totem identification that marked their soul and remained the name to which they answered when they went to the spirit world.

Because the great majority of the readers of this book were not born into clans or families that bear the names of animals, we shall expand on the strict defini-tion of "totem" as an animal representation of one's ancestral surname. If you have received an image of an animal medicine helper in a dream or a vision, we shall further anoint the power of that symbol of your spirit guide to become your totem animal in Dreamtime. In other words, if you have been shown that the bear is a symbol of your guide, the appearance of a bear in your dreamtime will be a signal to your Higher Self that a series of very important symbols will soon appear that will assist you in dealing with any problems that may be troubling you. We will call that animal your totem, and if you do not yet have a four-legged, a bird, or a reptile as your medicine guide, don't worry, we'll get you one.

Here is how a traditional Indian would obtain his medicine guide.

Silver Cloud, my mentor from the Winnebago tradition, was about thirteen, living in the Black River Falls
area of Wisconsin, when he went on his vision quest:

"We were tutored for many weeks on what to expect and what
would be expected of us. Then we were asked to go out into the
woods and pick a spot where there was a stream. We could not bring
any food with us, and it was forbidden to seek out berries or any other
kind of nourishment. We were also told that we must not seek shelter.
If it rained, we were to remain exposed to the elements. We were to
tire our bodies and continue to pray to Manitou, the Great Mystery, at
least three times a day. Always, most important, we were to pray for
our guide to appear.

"The main idea behind the rite of the vision quest is to exhaust the
physical body as completely and as quickly as possible. One of the
exercises that the tribal council suggested was that we find a place
where there were a lot of rocks, so that we might pick them up and
run with them from one place to another.

"After we had made a pile in one place, we could pick them up
and carry them back to the original place. Just keep on making a pile
one place, then pick them up and carry them back again--repeating the
process again and again, over and over.

"I understand now that the exercise was designed to enable us to
busy our conscious mind with a monotonous physical activity while
the subconscious mind was concentrating on the encounter with the
guide.

"After a while, when I was sitting or lying down to rest, I started
to see wildlife seeming to become friendlier. Soon, some creature
would approach me, as if to offer itself as a totem, a guide. I had a
chipmunk come up to me. A bird landed on my shoulder. A gopher
walked up to me as I rested. Even a badger approached me in a
friendly way.

"I was very hungry, and I knew that I could go back to the village
if I accepted one of these creatures as my guide. One of the elders
had warned us against this. He had said,'If you boys get hungry and
are afraid of staying out in the wilderness all alone, you will be
tempted to accept the first creature who approaches you as your
guide. But if you can endure, the Great Mystery, or some spirit in

human form, will appear and talk to you.'

"I spent twelve days fasting and awaiting my guide. I decided that I would endure and meet a spirit from the Great Mystery.

"I had many beautiful creatures approach me and offer themselves to me. Once a magnificent deer came up to me and allowed me to pet its neck and scratch its ears. I knew that the deer wanted to stay. I knew that it wanted to be my totem. I considered this for a long time. The deer is a fine totem to have.

"The medicine chief of the tribe had told us boys how to refuse a guide. He said that we should thank it for coming and tell it of is beauty, its strength, its intelligence. But tell it also that we were seeking one greater.

"On the twelfth day of my quest, a glowing, illuminated form appeared before me. Although it was composed primarily of light, it did have features and it was clothed in a long robe. 'You I have waited for,' I told it.

"And it replied to me: 'You have sought me, and you I have sought.' Then it faded away. But it had appeared to me as solidly and as real as you are.

"On the evening that each boy was to appear before the Winnebago council to tell of his experience and the manifestation of his guide, the elders and the chief accepted my guide as genuine. I don't think there was any way that any young boy could have fooled that tribal council. They knew when he had had a true and real experience--or when he had used something as an excuse to get back to the reservation and get something to eat.

"One important thing that we were taught: We must never call upon our guide until we had exhausted every bit of physical energy and mental resource possible. Then, after we had employed every last ounce of our own reserve, we might call upon our guide and it would appear."

In the early 1980s, I devised a guided visualization that simulated the vision quest which proved to be quite successful at Medicine Wheel gatherings and at Medicine seminars. This technique is reproduced in *Indian Wisdom and Its Guiding Power* [Whitford Press, Schiffer Publishing, co-authored with Sherry Steiger], and I recommend the process highly for those who would like to replicate as closely as possible the traditional Indian vision quest and the subsequent acquisition of a totem guide.

I received my totem animal in August of 1972 when Twylah Nitsch, the Repositor of Seneca Wisdom, did me the great honor of adopting me into the Wolf Clan of the Seneca tribe. My adoptive name is *Hat-yas-swas* (He Who Testifies), and I was charged with continuing to seek out and to share universal truths.

I feel very comfortable with the wolf as my totem, my spiritual medicine helper, and the symbol of my guide. I have more than a dozen sweatshirts and tee shirts which feature wolves in their design, and I have numerous paintings of wolves in my home and office. Wolves have appeared often in significant dreams to warn me of impending crises and to present me with symbols that have aided me in solving troublesome problems.

But what about those of you who say that you have as yet no totem animal and don't have the faintest idea how to acquire one?

A simple and direct method would be to adopt the totem animal that corresponds to your birthdate in the American Indian zodiac that was devised by Sun Bear and his Medicine Helper Wabun for their Medicine Wheel teachings and by popular Florida astrologer Dikhi Jo Mullen, who attended monthly Full Moon Pipe Ceremonies for a year. Find your birthdate below and see how the totem animal associated with it "feels" to you.

March 21 to April 19: The Red Hawk

Those born under the sun sign of the Red Hawk (which corresponds to Aries) are likely to be adventurous and assertive. Along with their creativity, they harbor a desire to be free and unencumbered. Those people closest to them may consider them to be a bit headstrong at times.

April 20 to May 20: The Beaver

Beaver people are industrious and hardworking folks who are generally blessed with good health. They cherish peace and security, and those born under this sign (which corresponds to Taurus) are thought to be loyal and stable.

May 21 to June 21: The Deer

Deer people are very often clever, talented individuals who have a knack for bringing their enthusiasm to their environment. Those born under this sign (which corresponds to Gemini) love change and seem to be almost constantly in motion.

June 22 to July 21: The Brown Flicker

Those born under this sign (which corresponds to Cancer) have a

Tlingit Raven mask

strong nesting instinct and are generally deemed good parents who provide lovingly for their children. Brown Flicker people also seem to have an ability to head problems off before they really begin.

July 22 to August 21: The Sturgeon

Sturgeon People (who correspond to Leos) have a great talent for teaching others. If they can avoid the tendency to be a bit too domineering, they are able to hide all their insecurities behind a positive approach to life.

August 22 to September 22: The Bear

Those born under this sign (which corresponds to Virgo) are usually slow and cautious, quiet and careful individuals. Bear people are generally no-nonsense types who do not tolerate deceit and insincerity in others.

September 23 to October 22: The Raven

Raven people (who correspond to Librans) are the sociable, talkative folks, full of nervous energy and fluctuating moods. They are usually very flexible and adapt well to new environments and circumstances.

October 23 to November 21: The Snake

Charismatic, but often difficult to understand, Snake people are most often thought of those who may delve too deeply into the mysterious and forbidden. Those born under this sign (which corresponds to Scorpio) have the ability to deceive, as well as charm.

November 22 to December 21: The Elk

Elk People are competitive and athletic individuals who often serve as teachers and coaches. Those born under this sign (which corresponds to Sagittarius) enjoy traveling and cherish their personal independence.

December 22 to January 20: The Snow Goose

Tradition is important to those born under this sign (which corresponds to Capricorn), and they search the past in order to find meaningful guidelines for the future. Hardworking folks with great stamina, they are cautious about making too many changes in their lives.

January 20 to February 18: The Otter

Although those born under this sign (which corresponds to Aquarius) can be thought unpredictable, they usually prove to be good-natured friends who seem truly to enjoy helping others. Otter people are often found in service occupations.

February 19 to March 20: The Cougar

Cougar people, very mystical in nature, are often artists, writers, and healers, who rely on their intuition to help them avoid trouble. Perhaps a bit too sensitive, those born under this sign (which corresponds to Pisces) are easily hurt by rejection and disapproval.

Cherokee mask of animal hides designed to lure animals
during the hunt.

If the totem animal associated with your birth date seemed to mesh with your sense of inner harmony, then you may feel perfectly at ease in accepting that creature as your totem. If for any reason you did not feel compatible with the totem indicated by the American Indian zodiac, here is a technique that may help you to find a spirit medicine helper who seems more appropriate.

Just before you lie down to fall asleep, repeat the following to yourself in a slow, confident, measured voice. Once again, if you wish, you may record the programming in your own voice, accompanied by the traditional Indian flute, classical, or New Age music.

"I am an aware being, ever evolving spiritually. I now seek my totem, the symbol of my guide, my Medicine helper. As I dream during the night, an aspect of my Essential Self shall remain aware that I am dreaming. During my dream, I know that I have the ability to manifest whatever it is that I wish. I know that I have the ability tonight to manifest the image of my totem animal. I know further that I have the ability to remember clearly the image of my totem animal when I awaken."

Permit yourself to fall asleep after you have read the programming aloud as often as you wish. If you have recorded the programming, fall asleep listening to the message and the relaxing music. Allow matters to proceed naturally. You will be pleasantly surprised how quickly and effectively this technique will work for you. However, if you do not succeed on your first try, do not be discouraged. Authentic spiritual growth can take time, especially if a serious study of Medicine ways are new to you.

Once you have received your totem animal, its appearance in any dream will serve as a signal to you that a series of symbols will follow its manifestation in the dream scenario. Pay close and careful attention to those symbols and signs, for they have been designed by your spiritual guidance to assist you in making important decisions on your earthwalk.

Project Healing
to Others and Yourself
in Your Dreams

Today, any illness is expensive. Long gone is the day of the country doctors who would drive miles to treat illness or deliver babies for a few dollars or a couple of dozen eggs. Today we have specialists, technicians, five-hundred-dollar-a-day hospital rooms, and medical bills that can bring the average working family to bankruptcy. Even to diagnose an illness and find out what is wrong with a person in the first place can require extensive hospitalization and the services of many specialists and technicians. The cost can mount to several thousand dollars in a few days.

Most doctors and medical personnel are hardworking, selfless individuals, who, God love them, are caught in a system that has careened out of control and threatens to harm both those who serve and those whom they would serve. What I will offer in this chapter is intended only to supplement regular medical attention, not to replace your family doctor. It is certainly nothing other than a desire to aid fellow humans in pain that inspired Medicine Priests to create the healing beam of the "magic crystal."

In experiments which a number of us conducted with healing, we sent gifted dreamers traveling through time and space to visit subjects in faraway locations. Once the healers were there in their spirit bodies, they saw the subjects in X-ray form, diagnosed their ailments and diseases, and, in cases where permission was given, removed the "black spot" of illness with the healing beam of the magic crystal.

Renaissance symbol of Regeneration employs the same concept of the Indians, who saw the snake shedding its skin as a sign that it could continually be born anew.

The technique was simple. Once the healer was placed into a deep sleep, we continued speaking to him, directing him to the subject. When we were certain that his spirit was truly there, the healer would see the subject in X-ray form and describe the areas that were dark with sickness. When the diagnosis had been made, he turned a beam from the magic crystal on the black areas and continued to shine healing light upon the dark spots until they disappeared.

In case after case, we were informed that significant healings had occurred. In one of our most dramatic healings, an army combat veteran was able to cancel a scheduled amputation of his battle-damaged feet because the magic crystal's beam had removed all the dark spots from the mutilated area. Although he had resigned himself to at least six months in a wheel chair before he had to begin the awkward process of learning to walk again, he was able to leave our experiment on his own motive power and to walk three miles in celebration. Today, many years later, he is still walking on the feet that orthodox medical science would have taken away from him.

As the shamans and Medicine Priests learned centuries ago, healing is as much an art as it is a science. One and one may always make two, but the same pill certainly does not work for every patient who ostensibly has the same disease. There are so many variables and subtle factors involved in true healing. The delicate relationship between doctor and patient, the patient's will to recover, the doctor's own confidence in his ability to accomplish the healing--all these factors and so many more remain forever beyond the elucidation of the laboratory.

Once again I stress that I am not suggesting that out-of-body diagnosis and healing from Dreamtime should replace the physician. I certainly wish to pose no threat to orthodox medical men, but I would like to offer them a challenge to investigate seriously certain alternative techniques that are provided in Medicine Power.

Here is the simple technique which you may use to assist your family doctor in accomplishing a more complete healing of yourself or others.

As an out-of-body, altered state technique, record the following in your own voice so that you may serve as the guide that directs you after you have placed yourself in a deep state of relaxation. Or, if you prefer, have a trusted friend or family member read the following and allow them to serve as your guide:

"You are so peaceful, so relaxed. You are lying in a very peaceful place that you feel is your special Medicine power place. You know that you are safe here, and that you may relax completely.

"You glance up into the blue sky and pick out the most attractive, wonderfully formed cloud that you can see; and as you look upward at the cloud, you feel even more deeply at peace. You know that you have the ability to soar through the sky, to fly higher than the clouds.

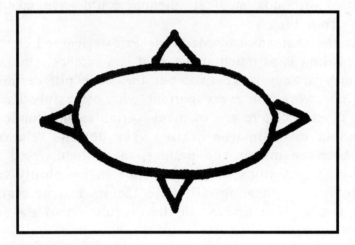

Pictoglyph of the
Great Mystery

You know that the Essential Self within you is free of Time and
Space. You know that you have the ability to travel anywhere you
wish...instantly. You know that you have the ability to heal others or
yourself. You know that you heal only with love, with no thought of
personal gain.

"And as you look up at the cloud, you are becoming more and
more relaxed. From this point on, any sound that you might hear will
not disturb or distress you. In fact, any sound that you might hear will
only place you deeper and deeper into a state of complete relaxation.
And as your body grows more relaxed and heavier, your spirit, your
Essential Self, grows freer and lighter. Freer...and lighter. Free of the
body. Lighter than air. Able to move faster than light speeds across
the heavens.

"And now you feel your spirit moving free of your body, free to
travel through Time and Space. Free to go to the home of
_____, who is in need of healing. At the count of three, you
will be present in spirit at the side of _____. One, moving
closer. Two, closer still. Three, you are in the presence of
_____.

"You have the ability to see _____ in X-ray form. You have
the ability to see all the places where the injury or disease has

affected _____. See those places in your X-ray vision as dark spots, black areas on _____'s body.

"Take your magic crystal out of your Medicine bag and activate it with your love energy. Send love to the crystal until it begins to glow with green healing light and begins to send out a beam of healing energy. The magic crystal will be ready at the count of three. One, beginning to glow. Two, becoming aglow with green healing light. Three, the healing beam is shining forth.

"Now direct the healing beam toward all the areas on _____'s body that show up as black spots. Keep shining until all the spots are gone. Keep directing the healing love energy until all the spots are clean and free of darkness and illness.

"When all the spots are gone, replace the magic crystal in your Medicine bag and know that you have the ability to return to your body. At the count of three, you will be back in your body feeling better than you have felt in weeks and weeks, in months and months. At the count of three, you will be back in your body and awaken filled with thoughts of love. One, coming awake. Two, more and more awake, feeling better than you have felt in months. Three, wide awake and filled with love!"

As a Dreamtime technique, read the following before you fall asleep at night; or as before, record the following in your own voice so that it is repeated several times as you are falling asleep.

"As an aware Medicine person whose mission is to serve and to help others, I know that I have the ability to heal myself and others. I know that I have the ability to travel through Time and Space and to appear in Dreamtime in the home of _____. As I manifest in the Dreamtime home of _____, I know that I have the ability to shine the healing light of my magic crystal on all dark places of injury and illness on the body of _____ and to remove all black spots from _____'s flesh. I know that I have the ability to see _____'s body in X-ray form and to shine my magic crystal on all the black spots that are revealed. I know that as an aware and loving Medicine person, I will shine my healing light on all the dark spots on _____'s body until they are clean, until all the black places are free of disease or pain. I will then sleep soundly, enveloped in love, until I awaken in the morning."

Learning to Interpret
Your Personal
Dream Symbols

As such great Medicine teachers as Silver Cloud have stated, everyone must learn to interpret his or her own dreams: "No one has ever been able to set down a strict code of dream interpretation or universal symbols that strictly apply to everyone--although wise ones have been trying to do just that for thousands of years. All attempts to label a specific symbol with only one meaning is bound to fail."

In the following section, I intend to succeed, rather than fail, by offering a number of *suggested* interpretations of various symbols as they may appear in your dream scenarios. I remain completely undogmatic in my assertions, and many of the proffered analyses are composites of interpretations that were given by a number of gifted shamans and Medicine people. In some cases, I have simply offered cross-cultural references regarding a particular symbol and pointed out the universality of its impact upon a wide range of civilizations, past and present.

I have also included biographical sketches of numerous chiefs and Medicine Priests who regularly manifest as spirit guides for contemporary men and women who walk the medicine path. In addition there are pictoglyphs aplenty from "talking rocks" throughout the Americas which you may feel free to apply to your

Medicine shields, bags, and any other personal items that seem appropriate to you.

Please, however, do not accept my interpretations for any of the symbols as the final word writ upon stone. I have intended them only as thoughts designed to stimulate your personal investigation of the limitless potential of Dreamtime and as energy that might prime your own spiritual fountains. Go into the silence of meditation and explore, study, and seek on your own. The rewards that you are capable of receiving are truly beyond measure.

ABDOMEN To dream of the abdomen is to give expression to expectations that you hold toward the future. If you are a man and dream of your abdomen swelling and becoming larger, you may be foreseeing honors and acclaim coming your way. The same may be true if you are a woman, but, of course, in your case you might also be foreseeing a coming pregnancy.

If the night vision portrays you having pains in the abdominal area, you may be giving "birth" to conditions that will prove favorable to you. If the dream depicts the pains being due to a belt about the waist that you are cinching too tight, you should spend time examining how you may be "choking" or "strangling" the potentially favorable happening from taking place.

ABDUCTION If a man sees himself being carried away by shadowy figures, the abduction may signify that a situation or an event that he has been planning will turn out well.

If a woman dreams of being abducted by strangers, she is likely to participate in a very important event that will prove to be very beneficial to her. If she knows the abductors, then she should spent some time in contemplating what role the players have in her current or past life situations. The people portrayed must be analyzed to determine whether they will demonstrate helpfulness or a hindrance in achieving the beneficial event.

ACOMA PUEBLO Akome means "people of the white rock," and their pueblo is perhaps the oldest inhabited American Indian settlement in the United States. Situated on a rock mesa approximately sixty miles west of the Rio Grande, the pueblo is essentially unchanged since Coronado's *conquistadors* visited there in 1540. If your dream guide should take you on a night journey to visit the Acoma Pueblo, you must have a great connection to the old ones who lived on this continent long ago.

ACORN To dream of gathering acorns is to foresee good luck and prosperity ahead due to your careful planning. If you envision yourself discovering a great *cache* of acorns, you may be about to receive a great windfall of wealth. You might even be in line to receive a legacy of riches from a friend or relative.

AGE A dream drama in which you seemed worried about aging may signify an approaching illness. If you dreamt about a spouse or lover growing older, you feel the need to grow closer to that individual. If your night vision focused on the age of a business associate, that person may be deceiving you in some way.

ALLIGATOR If you perceived yourself in a boat watching nervously the approach of several alligators, your dream guide is warning you to be very careful in some new procedure or speculation. If you are in the water and one or more alligators are approaching you, you may well be surrounded by enemies of a physical or spiritual nature.

ALTAR If the night vision has shown you discovering a hidden altar, you may be about to be surprised by the finding some lost money.

If you have seen yourself kneeing at an altar in earnest prayer, you may expect to have a secret desire soon fulfilled. If your prayer became jumbled and confused, you may be harassed by enemies before that cherished desire can manifest in the manner that you wish.

An altar for a traditional Indian could be constructed of many things--bowls, prayer sticks, pipes, rattles, feathers, animal skins--or it could simply be a buffalo skull. On some occasions, good clear springs were used for purposes of going into the silence and communing with the Great Mystery. Some altars were constructed directionally for the purpose of addressing spirits of the east, west, north or south.

Certain scholars have stated that an altar symbolizes the regenerative Earth Mother. A number of witch cults consider their altar to represent the womb from which all life emerges. Other traditions, such as those who emphasize the Goddess in their worship, see the object of their veneration as the "Altar of Heaven."

If you dream of your altar being destroyed by seen or unseen forces, be prepared to defend your beliefs and your life path.

If your dream guide shows you in the process of building a beautiful new altar, you may soon receive great financial rewards.

AMETHYST To have a good dream in which you admire an amethyst is to recognize that you are quite contented with the general flow of your life pattern.

If you are given an amethyst by someone, your dream guide is preparing you for some unexpected good news.

If you subsequently lose that gift of an amethyst, you are forewarned that an enemy is ambitiously seeking your destruction.

AMULET If you are placing an amulet anywhere on your person, your dream guide is advising you that you must soon make a very important decision.

Be certain to remember if there was a depiction of any totem animal on the amulet for additional clues to the correct interpretations of this symbol. If a stranger presented you with the amulet in your dream drama, beware of friends who are jealous of you.

If you have seen yourself buying or creating a new amulet, be cautious concerning spiritual attack by unseen opponents.

ANGEL [LIGHT BEING] To entertain an angel or Light Being in a dream very often signals happiness in love.

If you dream of opening the door of your home to an angel, you may well have dreamed of the advent of prosperity in your life. If more than one angel stands at your door in such a dream, you may be about to receive a substantial inheritance.

If you or a loved one has endured a long illness, the dream of an angel may indicate that the Final Passing to the land of the grandparents is about to occur.

If your dream guide creates a scenario in which you develop a close relationship with an angel, you will certainly be given great peace and a marvelous sense of well-being.

Pictoglyph of the "First Beings" before souls and humans created by the Great Mystery.

The belief of traditional Indians that each person had an individual guardian spirit or guide is shared by the ancient Greeks and by contemporary Christians. The Greeks and the traditional Indian also maintain that the spirit guide can appear in the form of the animal totem, should it choose to do so. Perhaps most Christians would agree that their guardian angel could influence or temporarily enter the body of an animal to work a physical miracle, should it choose to do so.

ANT You are about to enjoy a wonderful meal when you notice that the food is crawling with ants. Don't despair. In dream symbology, you will soon find yourself in a situation that will bring you great happiness.

If you dream that you are carefully observing a long stream of ants slowly moving a large object, you are being reminded of the virtues of perseverance and industriousness.

Amu was the name of the "Ant Clan" of the Pecos tribe in New Mexico.

ANTELOPE If the antelope is your totem animal, its appearance in your dream is a signal from your dream guide advising you to be alert to a series of important symbols that will assist you in making an important decision or will direct you to a better path in order to solve a problem that is vexing you.

If you dream of someone presenting you with footwear made of antelope hide, you will soon receive great wealth.

If you are handed a Medicine pouch made of antelope leather, be very cautious of being deceived.

APPARITION If your Dream Catcher has snared a night drama in which you have beheld the apparition of a deceased relative, you will quite likely soon receive good luck and prosperity.

If the apparition greeted you in a somber, but friendly, manner, you may expect to hear good news very soon.

If the apparition frightened you, you should be very mindful of your health for the next three or four days. Be especially judicious in your choice of nutrition.

Should there have been many apparitions, ghosts, or phantoms in your dream, practice strong Medicine discipline to remain in balance. If the entities were dressed

A mask of the Old Man of the Forest, designed, perhaps, to prevent children from straying too far away from the village.

in black, be on guard against situations that may offer temptations designed to lead you from the spiritual path. If the beings were garbed in white, be assured that great blessings are on their way to you from the spirit world.

If you should learn that your lover had a dream of a ghost or phantom on the same night that you experienced your vision of an apparition, be aware that the person whom you love may be hesitant about making a commitment to you.

If you are married and you discover that your spouse dreamed of an apparition on the same night that you perceived such a being, interpret the dual visitation as a warning against travel plans for the next few days.

Since one of the eight basic tenets of Medicine Power is a strong belief in a partnership with the world of spirits, it is wise to study carefully any dream in which a phantom or an apparition appears to you.

If the spirit being should simply appear, then disappear, remaining only long enough for you to be made aware of its presence, you are likely to receive happiness and a positive change of fortune.

If the ghost materialized long enough to speak with you, you should expect troubles to appear in your physical reality within a few days of the dream.

If a rather frightening apparition manifested before you in a startling manner, yet you exhibited no fear, your dream guide is demonstrating how easily you will handle a highly disagreeable event that is about to enter your life path.

Gray Robe:
An Apparition that Cares

For two centuries, the Navajo deep in the Red Valley of Arizona have been aided in time of peril by the strange apparition of a spirit entity that has come to be known as Gray Robe. Those who have experienced the aura of his being say that there is something gentle about the shadowy figure who appears and disappears after guiding their steps to safety in the face of what seemed sure calamity.

Not long ago, a white man named Winslowe, who ran a trading post in the twenty-two mile long Red Valley, told of the day when he was journeying to Tonalea for his twice-weekly mail pickup. He was accompanied by two aging Medicine men known as Naranza and Sagnetyazza, both practitioners of the sacred big rites.

Once the mail had been collected and sacked, the three men stayed until nearly 10 p.m. to visit with other traders before beginning their return journey.

As their car approached the descent of a 30-foot deep wash, Winslowe slowed for the steep grade. Suddenly both old men shouted in unison: "Stop! There stands Gray Robe in the sagebrush!"

Startled, Winslowe jammed on the brakes, killing the motor and rocking the vehicle to a halt. For a moment in the moon's bright light, he thought he saw a dim gray shape standing near the road. Both hands of the figure seemed to be motioning them to turn back.

Then, just as suddenly, there was nothing where the shadowy figure had been--only moonlight and the silvered sagebrush. In the eerie stillness that followed the appearance of the apparition, the men were clearly able to hear the roar of rushing water.

When they had crossed the area only a few hours earlier, it had been dusty dry under a cloudless afternoon sky. But now, swift floodwaters had swallowed the crumbling roadbed at the high points. Had the car gone a few more yards, it could have been washed away by the swift-moving current. Winslowe and the two Medicine men had been saved from an almost certain death by the helping hand of Gray Robe.

The legend of Gray Robe had its beginnings on a bitter cold November day in 1776 when Father Silvester Valez de Esdalante and his party were on an expedition led by Father Francisco Atanasio Domeniques. The band had left Santa Fe in late July, and by October they arrived in what is now the Arizona Strip country, searching for a crossing point in the Colorado River. The trek had been extremely arduous, and the members of the expedition were reduced to eating some of their pack animals in order to stay alive.

On November 7, the explorers were successful in finding a river crossing opposite the Navajo Mountain. Exhausted and without food, they hoped to obtain provisions from the friendly Havasupais who farmed the area to the south.

A wandering Navajo, however, halted the weary explorers from expending their failing energy by seeking out the Havasupais. The tribe had already harvested their crops and had gone into the mountains, bearing their food with them. Their remaining strength would be better spent, the Navajo advised, by taking refuge where they were and by foraging among the dry cornstalks for any ears that the farmers may have overlooked. In addition, the Navajo promised, his small band would share with the explorers whatever food they might spare.

Father Esdalante was overwhelmed by the Navajo man's providential intervention that had prevented the expedition from traveling further and starving to death. At the same time, the Navajos' willingness to share their meager food supplies touched him as an act of true Christian generosity toward strangers. As the folds of his gray robe flapped amidst the swirling snowflakes, he knelt and blessed the place and its people.

It was only a few months after the expedition had moved on toward Moquland that Gray Robe made his first appearance.

A young Navajo named Black Hat was traveling alone by starlight along the Red Valley Trail when his pony reared sharply in alarm at the appearance of a gray form standing just off the path. All of his senses alerted, Black Hat saw that the figure in gray was motioning for him to follow him through the heavy sagebrush.

Deciding to heed the man in the gray robe, Black Hat nudged his pony a few hundred feet from the trail. Here, the figure slowly turned, pointed to a rocky ridge, and indicated that the young Navajo should go there. Then the figure vanished.

At the rocky base of the ridge, Black Hat discovered an unconscious Indian who lay suffering from a badly broken leg. Gathering dry sagebrush, Black Hat started a signal fire which attracted a dozen Navajo who lived nearby. The man had been thrown from his horse. Had Gray Robe not brought help, he might easily have died.

When Black Hat sought to describe the man in the gray robe who had summoned him to the side of the badly injured man, certain men and women back in his village said that his words drew a picture of the man who had knelt to give the Christian blessing to the fields and the people of the Red Valley.

At another time, Gray Robe is credited with saving the life of a crippled woman who was alone and starving in an isolated hogan. Unable even to stand, she had given up hope that she would be found before death came.

Local legend says that it was Gray Robe who appeared at the hogan door and motioned for her to rise and to walk outside.

Miraculously, and without pain from her crippled legs, the woman followed the shadowy figure for nearly a mile to a place to rest beside a long-abandoned horse trail. Within moments of her safe delivery to this spot, the mysterious figure vanished.

A short while later she was found by a Navajo couple, who, for no explainable reason, had succumbed to an impulse to return home by the old trail instead of traveling their customary route. They took the old woman home and cared for her until she recovered.

Another story recounts the time when Gray Robe manifested twice to two lost sisters who had strayed from a summer sheep camp near Red Lake.

When a particularly violent sandstorm struck sud-

denly, the two little shepherds had been unable to
follow the sheep home through the stinging, blinding
sand. Searchers who braved the terrible winds and tear-
ing sand also became lost, but they continued to battle
the storm in the hope of finding the sisters.

After the winds had subsided, Stone Leg, one of the
searchers, found a sign that the little girls might have
survived the storm when he discovered small moccasin
tracks in freshly rippled sand. Responding to his call
for help, men on horseback rode in ever-widening
circles, shouting for the children to answer them.

By nightfall, all but one man, a white trader named
Joe Lee, had given up the hunt. Lee headed alone across
the valley toward White Horse Mesa until he reached
the south side of the spring called Naschito. Here he
saw the form of a tall man in a gray robe holding out
both hands to him, then pointing to the ground at his
feet.

Blinking his eyes in astonishment, Lee saw the approaching forms of the two lost little girls. Walking
slightly ahead of them was the figure of Gray Robe, an
entity that Lee had long attributed to Indian superstition and folklore.

When they heard the clattering hooves of his horse,
the girls turned toward Lee, then raised their arms and
their voices in salutation. Gray Robe watched silently
for a moment, then disappeared.

After the girls had taken sips of the water from the
canteen that Lee handed them, he hoisted them to his
saddle and the three of them began the joyful journey
back to the Navajo village.

Once they had rested, the sisters told their adventure
to a ring of eagerly listening friends and family members. Gray Robe had appeared to them soon after the
blinding storm had blotted out all signs of their familiar world. Calming them with reassuring gestures, he
led them to the safety of a small cave where they
waited out the storm.

After the last howls of wind had died down, the
girls intended to start for home; but they had become

confused by the newly accumulated sand banks, and they set off in the wrong direction. Then, weakened by the ordeal, they collapsed to the ground.

Once again the apparition of Gray Robe materialized before them. This time he knelt beside them and appeared to be praying in the manner of the Christian missionaries. After he had blessed them, they found new strength, and they were able to follow him until Mr. Lee, the white trader, had found them.

The girls' father, who had lived all his life in the area, did not know of the cave to which Gray Robe had led his daughters to safety. But when he followed their directions, he discovered the place of refuge.

Joe Lee, a man who had a certain scholarly bent, asked an elderly Navajo sand painter who he thought Gray Robe was. "Do you think that he is the ghost of that priest who blessed the Red Valley back in the 1700s?"

The old man shrugged. "None of us know who Gray Robe is. None of us know why he acts as our protector. It is enough that he does."

APPLE If you enjoyed a large, juicy apple in your dream, you are about to participate in a pleasant event that will present you with a most favorable outcome.

If you were eating sour apples, your dream guide is trying to show you that you are following a course of action that will soon cause great trouble for yourself.

If you saw yourself planting an apple seed that overnight matured into a rich, fruit-bearing tree, you will begin more and more to enjoy the positive results of your labors.

Eve's fruit of knowledge is very often represented in traditional Christianity as the apple. In the ancient traditions of Goddess worship, the sacred fruit of immortality is the apple. The old Norse held the apple to be symbolic of the soul's resurrection. The mystical Avalon of King Arthur's resting place is translated as "Apple-land."

On the level of the psyche, an apple a day can keep

more than the doctor away. To dream of possessing a golden apple or an apple larger and richer in color than others is to foresee a time of spiritual illumination approaching. Focus on the imagery and be prepared to receive the enlightenment when the special moment is offered to you.

ARROW To be struck by an arrow in your dream could very likely mean that you are about to experience misfortune caused by someone whom you do not suspect is an enemy.

If you pick up a quiver and find it full of arrows, be advised that friends whom you trusted may be working against you.

If you fit an arrow to your bow and it suddenly breaks before you are able to send it soaring, you may be about to suffer a failure in your business affairs or in your love life.

The Medieval sign of the spear or sword denoted that life was an extended pilgrimage during which the pilgrim may have to defend himself against the forces of evil. For the American Indian, the pictoglyph of the arrowhead symbolized that life is an extended quest on which the spiritual warrior may have to defend himself against the machinations of negative beings.

Sacred Arrows of the Cheyenne

The early white settlers, missionaries, and soldiers may have regarded many of the sacred objects of the American Indian shamanistic tradition as no more than bits of stick or stone. To the shaman and the people whom he served, however, these items of Medicine represented the very essence of their survival in a world that seemed at times to be unceasingly hostile toward them.

That one tribe may come to covet the sacred objects of another, especially if those objects are thought to possess exceptionally strong Medicine, is graphically illustrated in curious contest between the Cheyenne and the Pawnee over a bundle of sacred arrows. The struggle began in the Platte River valley during the early 1830s and grew with great intensity and increasing passion-- for the Cheyenne believed that the bundle of sacred Medicine arrows held their destiny as a nation.

According to both tribes, the blood feud began when their hunting parties clashed over a buffalo herd near the sweeping hills above the Platte River. War seemed inevitable; and while the drums of death began their ominous beat, warriors in each village began to make preparations to strike first *coup* and to fight bravely.

In the Pawnee camp, an elderly man named Racing Elk struggled to his feet from his sick bed and wrapped his robes about him to cover the terrible sight of the great sores upon his body. The old one told his kinsmen that they must take him to the place where they would fight the Cheyenne. Since he knew that he was dying, he would kill the enemy and fight like a warrior until his bow was silenced and he had found a warrior's death.

Out of respect for the old man, who had once been a mighty chief, members of his family carried Racing Elk and his weapons to the crest of the hill where the approaching battle would most likely begin. When the Pawnee attacked the waiting Cheyenne, the old man smiled grimly and fixed an arrow to his bow string.

As the fighting raged on, few warriors from either side paid the old one much heed. His eyes and his arms were not what they once had been, and his arrows flew wide of their mark.

But then a most remarkable thing occurred. Strong Bear, the warrior entrusted by the tribal council of the Cheyenne to carry the four sacred medicine arrows into battle, happened to come near the feeble old warrior. With a sudden burst of strength that nearly drained him of his life, Racing Elk, the ancient Pawnee, reached out and snatched the sacred medicine bundle from the startled Cheyenne warrior.

Those Pawnee nearest the old one rushed to his aid and were astonished to perceive the great trophy that he had captured. Shouting triumphant war cries, the Pawnee closed ranks around the captor of the sacred medicine bundle and beat back the furious attacks that the Cheyenne mounted to recapture the sacred arrows.

Fighting with a kind of ecstatic courage, the Pawnee drove off the desperate Cheyenne and returned jubilantly to their camp, singing a war song in honor of the old warrior who had stolen the enemy's power from them in one remarkable act of bravery. The celebrating Pawnee elevated Racing Elk--who had only wished to meet his death with dignity--to the rank of a tribal hero. As a special token of honor, he was awarded one of the medicine arrows that he had seized from the enemy.

The bloodied Cheyenne were as despondent as the Pawnee were elated. Although the family of Strong Bear would mourn him, they were glad for his sake that he had been killed attempting to regain the sacred arrows. Great would have been his shame if he had lost the medicine bundle and held on to his life.

When the Cheyenne Medicine priests heard of the loss of the sacred arrows, they issued a grave warning: "Unless the sacred arrows are returned to the Medicine lodge, great evil will befall all of the tribe."

Driven to a frenzy by the loss of their most sacred totem, the Cheyenne initiated night raids against the Pawnee camp that accomplished nothing. A series of skirmishes near the Pawnee camp resulted in a series of defeats for the Cheyenne. In desperation, they set trap after trap to snare Pawnee chiefs to exchange for the arrows; but always, as if by magic, the Pawnee eluded the snares and left the luckless Cheyenne gnashing their teeth in mounting frustration.

Blackfoot Medicine Shield

When neither force of arms nor ambush seemed to prevail, the Cheyenne turned to guile, a subtle art at which they were acknowledged as masters on the plains.

Wearing friendly faces that masked their hatred and their frustration, a Cheyenne delegation arrived at the Pawnee camp under a sign of truce.

"We are not certain that you have our sacred arrows," Burnt Tree, the Cheyenne spokesman began, "but we have been searching the area for them. They are not of great importance to us, but we do have a small attachment to them, and we might be willing to trade a few ponies for their return."

"How many ponies?" Horse that Charges, the Pawnee chief, wanted to know.

"Are the arrows really in your possession?" Burnt Tree countered.

"Oh, yes, we have them," Horse that Charges replied with a smug smile of immense satisfaction.

"We need proof before we speak further," Burnt Tree said.

Horse that Charges shrugged and motioned to Blue Hand, the war chief, to remove one of the arrows from beneath a buffalo robe and to allay any doubts that the Cheyenne might have that the Pawnee had stolen their sacred medicine.

With a whoop of delight, a Cheyenne warrior who had stood to Burnt Tree's right, seized the arrow from Chief Blue Hand and fled like a startled deer before the stunned Pawnee could collect their wits and give chase. Burnt Tree and the remaining Cheyenne scoundrels made good their escape during the ensuing wild hubbub that followed the warrior's daring snatch.

Sorely chagrined by the Cheyenne's treachery, the angry Pawnee could not believe their eyes when yet another Cheyenne delegation appeared at the camp's edge, also pleading a truce.

The new group of Cheyenne, under Chief Standing

Eagle, professed outrage at the duplicity of renegade members of their tribe, who, under Chief Burnt Tree had violated the truce so shamelessly by running off with the sacred arrow without redeeming the pledge of many ponies that had been offered as ransom.

"For this act of treachery, we must double the number of fine horses that we had intended to give you for the return of those arrows." Chief Standing Eagle paused, as if personally disinterested in his task as diplomat. "I don't know why we bother so over these arrows. It is only a few of our women who place some foolish value upon them."

The cunning Standing Eagle stifled a yawn, then seemed to rouse his senses to repeat an offer given to him by others. "If you will humor these silly women by returning the arrows, then honor us by sending a group of warriors back with us to our village--and they will all ride back on fine horses."

Proving that greed will nearly always mute reason, the Pawnee council agreed to send a group of warriors who would follow the Cheyenne on foot and return the sacred arrows to their medicine lodge. After all, the Pawnee council argued, the arrows meant nothing to them--and their long-standing enemy was willing to make them wealthy with horse flesh. Besides, they would have the last laugh, as the Cheyenne believed that they would be receiving three arrows, rather than two. They were unaware that Racing Elk had been awarded one of the sacred arrows for his brave capture of the medicine bundle.

As the Pawnee warriors trudged wearily behind the mounted Cheyenne, one of the rascal braves made what seemed to be a selfless gesture to the Pawnee chosen to carry the remaining medicine arrows.

"You are tired from carrying the bundle and your weapons," the Cheyenne said solicitously. "Here, ride my horse and make your burden lighter. I will walk for a while in your stead."

There seemed no ulterior motive in the offer, and the Pawnee warrior accepted with gratitude the opportunity to give his aching arms a chance to rest.

As the journey continued, the thoughtful Cheyenne renewed his offer a number of times; and he was even considerate enough to hold the bundle of sacred arrows while his new Pawnee friend mounted the horse.

It was during just such an exchange of riders that the cunning Cheyenne's treachery was revealed. As the Pawnee bundle bearer made ready to mount, he suddenly found himself sitting only on air. The thoughtful enemy to whom he had given momentary possession of the arrows had bolted the horse from beneath him, jumped on its back himself, and thundered off with the treasured arrows that the Pawnee had wrested from them. The deceitful warrior's flight was the signal for the rest of the Cheyenne band to spur their mounts forward.

Within moments, the horseless Pawnee were left to shout ancient curses at a whirlwind of dust.

Angered once again by such bold treachery, the Pawnee took comfort in the fact that their enemy had actually regained only one of their sacred arrows in the medicine bundle that the warrior carried. Just before the ill-fated journey began, the war chief Blue Hand had wisely hidden one of the Cheyenne medicine arrows in a place known only to himself. And, of course, another of the sacred arrows lay securely in the tent of Racing Elk to whom it had been awarded as a prize for his daring. The Cheyenne had thus regained only two of their sacred arrows--and each one by deceit. By such reckoning, the Pawnee consoled themselves, the Cheyenne medicine remained only half powerful.

But when the footsore Pawnee returned to their camp, they learned the awful truth of how ruthless the vengeful Cheyenne could be. The village lay in ashes. Those who had been left behind had been hacked to death by a second party of Cheyenne who had struck while their tribesmen lured the Pawnee away with the promise of many ponies.

Racing Elk, who had bravely reached out to take the Cheyenne medicine bundle, had been murdered in a particularly brutal fashion. The arrow that he had been awarded was gone.

Numbed with rage and sorrow, Chief Blue Hand vowed that the deceitful Cheyenne would never again see the fourth magic arrow--and he kept his promise by taking the whereabouts of the relic with him to his grave.

For the Cheyenne, who had tried every resource at their disposal to return all of the sacred arrows to their medicine lodge, the failure to recover the fourth arrow was seen as a sign that they would never again regain their supremacy on the plains.

As misfortune followed misfortune, the Cheyenne could only shake their heads sadly over dwindling campfires and recount that one fateful moment when an old man who had come to a battle field to die with dignity had reached out and changed the course of a proud nation's history.

ASHES A dream of walking through mounds of ashes may be alerting you to be careful before you lose something of great value to you through your own carelessness.

If you should see yourself paying respect to the cremated ashes of a relative, your dream guide is informing you that if you stay on the proper life path, you will enjoy a long and fruitful life.

AX The ax presents a universal symbol of bravery. To dream of yourself walking along a path carrying your ax is a strong Medicine admonition that you have the necessary courage to conquer whatever dangers and hazards may lie ahead of you.

If you notice that your ax is rusty or damaged, you

The ax is a universal symbol of bravery

are being warned to maintain a steady discipline and to carry the law of love in your heart--or you may suffer a great loss of fortune.

Should your night vision depict a friend approaching you with an ax, be advised that he or she may soon be in danger.

If you perceive strangers gathering axes, be alert that your own life may be in jeopardy.

If it is your enemies you see holding their axes, understand that it is quite likely to be impossible to come to an agreement with them, and you are in for anxiety and trouble.

A woman who dreams of a large, over-sized ax is being shown that her devotion to the Medicine path of love is going to be rewarded by the appearance of a man who is truly worthy of her depth of character. Should the dreamer be already wed or joined with a significant other, the ax symbolizes a renewal of personal commitment on the part of the loved one.

A man who dreams of a large, over-sized ax or an ax that has been allowed to become chipped or rusted is being warned by his guide that he is about to have love problems unless he pays attention to important details in his relationship.

Before the white man introduced iron ax heads to the Indian, warriors carried axes that weighed from one to six pounds--with some as heavy as thirty pounds. They were most often fashioned from granite or other hard rock.

The ax has been accepted as a symbol of the power of Light since the most ancient of times. Some scholars have theorized that primitive humans saw with their own eyes the mighty "ax stroke" of lightning from the heavens split great trees with one sudden blow. The ax, then, is a great symbol of the earthly pilgrim's ability to overcome the powers of darkness. The sign of the battle ax is equivalent to the sword, hammer, or cross.

And, some authorities speculate, the depiction of the double ax is a more ancient symbol than the single ax, as the earliest of axes were most likely double-edged stones bound to the end of a stout stick.

The Tau cross forms an ax, the symbol of the Forces of Light.

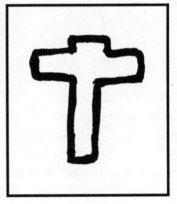

BABY If your guide has shown you a dream in which you encounter a beautiful baby, you may usually accept this symbol as a preview of great happiness.

If you are single woman dreaming of having a baby, you should be prepared for an act of sorrow entering your life. If you are married, you may expect happiness to bless your life path. If you are a married woman already pregnant, you are foreseeing continued success in a loving relationship.

A dreamer of either sex who observes a baby of obvious intelligence is being given a symbol of new friends of a trustworthy nature who are about to enter the flow of earth-plane existence. If the dreamer should behold a baby of uncommon ugliness, the guide is displaying a symbol that indicates misfortune ahead.

If the dream drama shows you a baby alone on its bed, you should be aware that this sign warns that you are being watched by someone with decidedly evil intentions. If the baby appears to be ill, you may soon hear of a family member who is suffering from a serious illness.

BADGER The Zuni regarded the badger as the younger brother of the bear, recognizing his strength and his stout heart, but faulting him for what they considered a will much weaker than his burly "older brother." The badger was the guardian and master of the region of the South in the Zuni cosmology. Because his coat was ruddy and evenly marked with stripes of black and white, they saw the creature as standing between night and day with the color of summer.

If your dream catcher seizes a vision of a badger, you may be about to begin a project that will burden you with a great deal of work.

If you have seen yourself catching a badger and subduing it, you will probably be the joyful recipient of good fortune.

On the other hand, should others somehow catch the badger that managed to elude you, be cautious of your enemies hatching a plot against you.

If the badger is your totem animal, your guide is advising you to be alert to a series of important symbols within the dream that will assist you in making an important decision or will direct you to a better path in order to solve a problem that is vexing you.

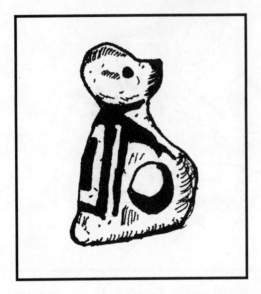

Zuni badger
fetish.

BAT The Medicine of most tribal shamans regards the bat as an evil omen. It is important to take careful notice of the color of the night-flying creature that your Dream Catcher has caught in its ethereal net. If the bat is a very black one, you may expect quarrels and unpleasantness right around the next corner. If its color should be gray, things are going to get easier for you in the near future. If its fur is pure white, you may take this color as an omen that the illness of a loved one is soon to leave.

Should the dream scenario depict you surrounded by dozens of bats with their wings flapping like thunder in your ears, be prepared for a death within your family.

If the bat is your totem animal, your dream guide is sending you an alert to watch for a series of symbols within the dream that will aid you in problem-solving or will provide clues to information that has been eluding you.

BEADS Before the white traders brought glass beads to the tribal villages, the Indians fashioned their beads out of shells, teeth, seeds, claws, wood, bird beaks, bones, and various minerals.

In many cases the arrangement of the beads and the choice of their color conveyed a message. Black beads signified war or death; white, peace and prosperity.

The Delaware people used to send "letters" to friends in other villages by means of strings of beads. The knot on the cord provided information concerning the starting point of the communication or the name of the person sending it. The end of the message was strung first so the beginning of the letter was composed of the first beads to meet the recipient's fingers as he or she unrolled the string.

If you have dreamed of having purchased a large supply of beads, you should be cautious of a number of false friends who care little for your best interests.

If your dream guide portrayed your string of beads breaking and scattering individual beads about the ground, you were being warned that recent ill-advised acts of yours have begun to cost you a significant portion of your reputation. On the other hand, should you have caught the beads before they fell, then carefully counted their number, you will be able to overcome the loss of your reputation and emerge virtually unscathed.

A dream in which you have found a hidden cache of beads is designed to warn you of forthcoming misery and pain.

BEAR The bear is among the most highly revered of all totem animals, and many Medicine Priests have adopted "bear" as a part of their name. The spirit of the bear, according to traditional Indian belief, never dies.

Like the people of the tribal villages, the bear was able to live on fish, flesh, or berries. The bear was known for its great love of honey, and its keen sense of smell seemed able to detect the sweet treasure of a bee hive at a great distance. The Indians watched in awe as

the lumbering giant ripped the honey from the hive without fear of being stung. The people from the villages also knew that the bear was aided in its quest for honey by long, formidable claws in its forepaws, each capable of independent movement, each curved in a fashion similar to the eagle's talons.

When the bear left its dwelling place to hunt for its sustenance, the Indians noted how it sauntered in a leisurely manner, its huge feet placed flat upon the ground and turned slightly inward, thereby causing the forest giant to walk in a peculiar movement. Although its head was of impressive proportions, its eyes were small and red, set in the large, hairy triangle of its head.

Often the bear would stand upright on its two hind feet and appear very much like a stout, powerfully built man with short, bandy legs. In such a position, the bear could attack its enemies, striking at the head and the belly with devastating results.

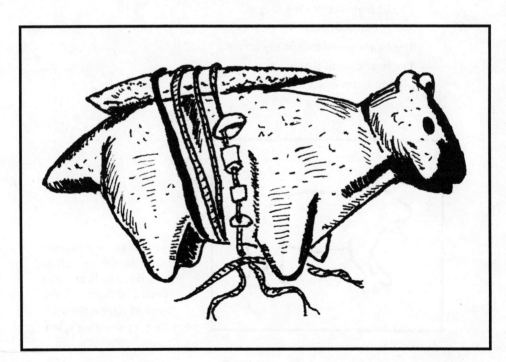

Zuni bear fetish.

Hunters from the various tribes were struck by the peculiarly sad whining moan that a bear would emit when struck by a mortal wound. Triumphant bowmen confessed to feeling compassion when they heard that pitiful cry as the forest giant breathed its last.

At the same time that the hunter might notice his prey's humanlike qualities, he was also keenly aware that the behemoth was very cunning and very strong. To kill the monster required a superior achievement. To ensure his success, the hunter relied upon his Medicine power. He would draw a figure of the bear with a line from its mouth to its heart. Then, by chanting magic words, the hunter envisioned himself gaining power over the great heart of the massive four-legged creature.

One such chant, an ancient one often attributed to the Chippewa, goes like this:

Hear the power in my voice.
My swiftness and strength is like that of the eagle.
The bear shall obey my magic.
A serpent shall enter his vitals.
The bear cannot escape my arrow.
The bear cannot flee my magic.
My Medicine is strong.

For many of the ancient tribes of Europe, as well as America, the bear was a symbol of the deity, the Great Mystery, the self-existent, everlasting spirit.

Among the ancient tribes of Europe, the Nordic warriors known as the "Berserkers" wore bearskin shirts into battle in dedication to the Goddess Ursel, the She-Bear. To the old Norse, the bear was a great martial artist; and the she-bear protecting her cubs was the most fierce creature under the Northern lights. To wear a bearskin shirt was to absorb the bear's great fighting spirit and its enormous endurance and strength.

If the bear is your totem animal, its appearance in your dream is a signal that your spirit guide is advising you to be alert to important symbols which will appear in your dream drama and which will assist you in making an important decision or will set you on a better path to solving a problem that is troubling you.

If you view a bear in a cage, you may expect to achieve success in the future.

Should you see yourself surrounded by many bears, be concerned that people are gossiping about you. If the dream depicts a bear attacking you, you may soon see the gossip becoming persecution. If you drive off the bear that is attacking you, you will eventually put those who plot against you in their place. Should you persist and kill the bear in your dream, you will achieve a major victory over your enemies.

Grandmother Twylah, Repositor of Wisdom for the Seneca, states that if you dream of a bear that stands before you on its hind feet, seeming to listen with only one ear and to see with only one eye, inwardly crying in silent despair, you have perceived a symbol that represents your loss of self-respect. Only you can change this sad and lonely feeling, and you should enter the Silence to receive instructions from the Great Mystery.

If you dream of eating bear meat, you are being warned that you may experience a long illness.

If your guide shows you a dream in which you have become transformed into a bear, you will soon receive sad news.

If you perceive a bear dancing on its hind legs, you are soon to be tempted into making unwise speculations.

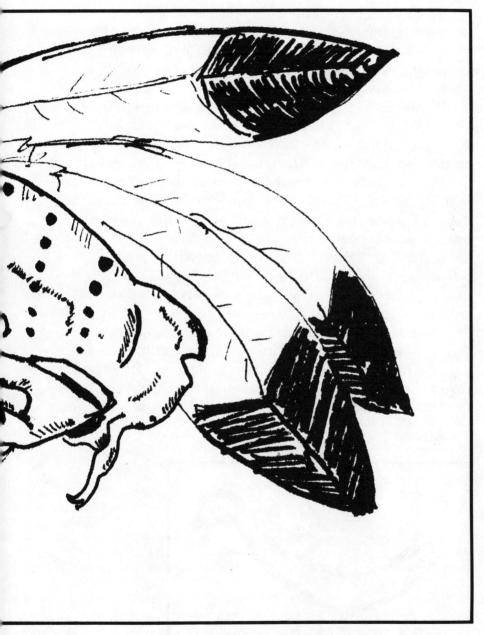

Bear skull painted for Medicine ceremonies

BEE A children's song among the eastern tribes focuses on the industrious insect's handicap in having only one stinger with which to defend itself:

> The poor little bee/That lives in a tree,/ The poor little bee,/That lives in a tree,/Has only one arrow/In his quiver.

Grandmother Twylah of the Seneca says that the bee is the symbol of an industrious, selfless, self-sufficient individual who can deal with great success in a wide range of activities.

If you should dream of a bustling beehive full of buzzing bees, you envision the abundance and wealth that is destined to be yours. Should the beehive be empty, prepare for a life relatively devoid of riches.

If your guide has created a painful scenario in which you are stung by many bees, you should keep a careful eye on friends and business associates and be on guard against being double-crossed.

If the dream drama has you menaced by bees but remaining untouched by the "single arrow in their quivers," you have been given a sign of success in your love relationship.

Should the dream have portrayed a swarm of bees flying into your home environment, be cautious of enemies who may cause you personal damage. However, if that swarm of invading bees should make honey in your home, you will triumph over those who would do you ill.

Bird pictoglyph.

BIRD In the eyes of ancient humans of all tribes, there are few creatures more likely to prompt worshipful thought than the winged ones of the air. The seemingly supernatural ability to soar high into the sky while leaving all two-leggeds and four-leggeds fixed forever below on the Earth Mother served as a creative stimulus for art, poetry, music, and religion.

From the very earliest of times, bits of sculpture, pictoglyphs, and etchings on pottery fragments reveal what appears to be a universal belief that birds ushered the soul of the deceased to a higher dimension of reality. The traditions of ancient Europe, as well as the shamanic metaphysics of the Americas, also held that the souls themselves could on occasion assume the form of birds. It is interesting to recognize that the Latin word *aves* could mean both birds and ancestral spirits-- or angels or ghosts.

Early European representation of a good, or holy, spirit expressed in the eagle.

Shamans throughout the world have "soul-traveled" as a bird while in a trance state. If the actual shape-change did not occur, the Medicine Priest would envision his spirit traveling in the company of a guardian bird.

Throughout the mighty empires of the Maya and the Inca, the hummingbird, primeval entity of the Elder World, is the symbol of the departed warrior. The artwork of these ancient craftsmen repeatedly displays the symbol of a pair of wings to serve as a suitable emblem for the unseen transit of the human soul.

The Holy Spirit is portrayed in Christian art as assuming the form of a dove. It has been said that when Indians of a certain tribe first saw the figure of a dove in a Roman Catholic chapel, they asked immediately if the winged-one was the Christians' Thunderbird.

Crude American
Indian representation of
the Thunderbird.

The symbol of the eagle is used, as well, to represent the Holy Spirit; and the Hebrews also employed the form of the eagle, along with the bull and the lion, to symbolize the Divine Being. The Scandinavians respected a mythological eagle that dwelt upon the branches of the sacred tree Yggdrasil.

In a number of the Eastern tribes, a Medicine Priest with accurate powers of prophecy was depicted in pictoglyphs with the heads of two hawks, together with plumage, attached to his shoulders. The beaks were drawn turned inward, as if in communication with the priest. If the prophet was believed to be one who used his abilities to accomplish good, three plumes were

Pictoglyph of a Medicine prophet
who used his powers for good.

drawn on each side of the head. If he were deemed un-
just and working for the dark side, there would be but
three plumes--and these all placed on one side.

The hawk was nearly as revered as the eagle in the
cosmology of the Indian Medicine priests. Some believed
that the hawk had the supernatural ability to "stay
long on the wing" and to be able to fly directly to the
land of spirits.

There are many birds that might be selected as powerful totem animal helpers. If you have perceived an image of your particular totem in your dream, then you are being alerted to be on watch for a series of important symbols that will aid you in making an important decision or will assist you to stand firm on the Medicine path.

To dream of birds flying in formation high in the sky above you is to receive a symbol of prosperity approaching you.

If you have dreamt of birds being caught and put into a cage, you will receive poor returns on a recent investment.

Should your dream guide have shown you scenes of birds fighting one another, you are being told to make a change in your business relationships. Perhaps you should seek other employment.

If you have glimpsed birds in their nest, you have been given a pleasant symbol of family happiness. Should all the birds have been asleep, however, you must be alert to a possible deception on the part of someone who will claim to bring you important news of a matter for which you have long awaited word. If the nest was empty, you must set about terminating troublesome business affairs.

Grandmother Twylah, Repositor of Wisdom for the Seneca, advises that to dream of a chirping bird is to receive an announcement of an event or a discovery that will bring great joy to you. A bird that faces east is a dream symbol that you are about to take a trip or to make a very important decision. A bird that sits high in a tree represents lofty ideals.

If you have been shown a nest full of bird's eggs, you will likely soon be the recipient of a great deal of money. If baby birds hatched while you observed the eggs, you will hear good news within a very few days. If a predator should suddenly manifest and eat the bird's eggs, you will soon be changing your personal environment in a dramatic fashion.

If you have witnessed the birth of an eagle in your dream, you are assured of a very prosperous future.

Grandmother Twylah has said that to dream specifically of a blackbird is to receive a signal that there will soon be a change in your learning experiences. Before effective growth can occur, however, a conflict needs to be understood.

BLACK HAWK Born in what is now Illinois in 1767, Black Hawk was a great leader of the Sac and Fox tribes. Although he is remembered in the white history texts as a war chief, Black Hawk tried always to walk the pathway of peace.

In 1804, summoned by the great white chiefs to St. Louis, representatives of the Sac and Fox succumbed to flattery, rum, and whiskey and ceded all their tribal lands east of the Mississippi. In 1812, Black Hawk fought on the side of British, hoping for better treatment from their officers and for the return of the Sac and Fox land if the Redcoats won.

After the defeat of the British, Black Hawk returned to the land west of the Mississippi where his people had been pushed by the whites, who were ever ravenous for Indian land. Finally, after suffering twenty years of humiliation and mistreatment, the 50-year-old Black Hawk promised to lead his people back to their ancestral lands.

Black Hawk, the great war chief, planned no armed conflict. Believing most whites to be people of conscience, he was convinced that his well-esteemed powers of oratory could persuade the farmers and townsfolk in western Illinois that he and his tribe and been wronged and that they should return the land on which they had settled to the Sac and Fox, the rightful owners. The whites' answer to the chief's eloquent plea was to mobilize a well-armed militia to march at once against the Indians.

Even though the Sac and Fox fought valiantly against overwhelming odds, the ill-fated Black Hawk war lasted only a few months. In August of 1832, just as Black Hawk was leading the tattered remnants of his Warriors back into Iowa to surrender, an enthusiastic band of militia met the Sac and Fox and killed most of them with a withering barrage of gunfire. Black Hawk died on October 3, 1838

If you should have received images of Black Hawk as a spirit helper or as guide who will offer inspiration and wisdom, you may be receiving a message to persevere in the face of overwhelming odds, but to trust in a balance of reason and action.

BLANKET Although contemporary homes enjoy displaying Indian blankets as wall pieces or rugs, to the traditional Indian the blanket was his one nearly indispensable belonging. The blanket was utilized as a body wrap, as a bed, as a door covering, as a partition within the lodge or tipi, as a bag for carrying food and other materials, and as a shelter on the trail--to name just a few of its uses.

If your guide has portrayed you buying a number of new blankets, you should sadly anticipate a loss of money.

If you are depicted as patching up an old blanket, you will soon be seeing an improvement in your economic condition.

If the dream scenario has you wrapping up in an old, tattered blanket, good news and good fortune is on its way to you.

BOAT Stereotypically, the Indian boat is thought of as the birchbark canoe or the dugout, which was simply a good-sized log that had been hollowed out by burning or by chopping. The birchbark canoe was popular among the northeastern tribes due to the availability of the birch tree and the easy accessibility of its bark. On the western plains, where trees were not as plentiful, river travel was negotiated by "bull-boats," tub-like craft covered with tightly woven animal skins.

To dream of yourself in a canoe, dugout, or other boat is to affirm that you intend to achieve your goal in life. If the water is smooth, fortune will come easy. If the waves become choppy, you will be liable to face many difficulties before your success is achieved.

Should you have seen yourself falling from the boat into the water, your guide may be telling you to abandon ship before the troubles become too many for you to overcome. If the craft overturned and sent you

sprawling into the stream, be advised that an enemy is
seeking to overthrow you from your present position in
life.

If you were in the canoe with a loved one, be on
guard against those who would seek to rob your of your
love or to breakup your relationship.

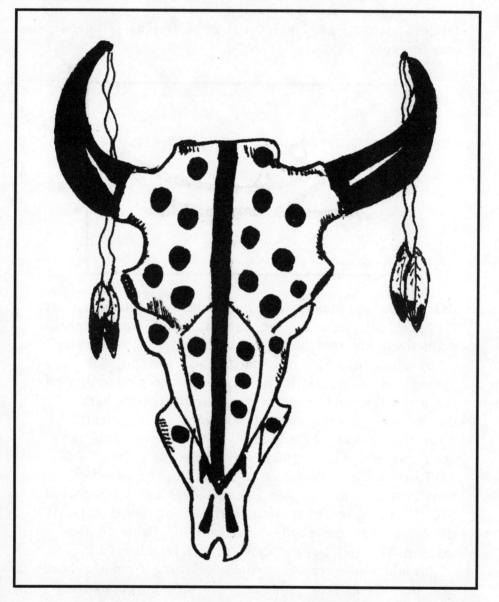

Buffalo skull decorated for Medicine rituals.

BUFFALO The buffalo, or bison, roamed the plains of the western United States and ranged as far east as the Allegheny Mountains. To the plains Indian the buffalo was a great symbol of the continuation of their life force and their life style. When the powerful beast was slain, the Indian used every part of the body--the meat, the blood, the hide, the sinew, the horns, the hooves-- even, some say, its dying breath.

From ancient Babylon and Crete to the plains of Nebraska and the Dakotas, the great bull represents the male aspect of the creator, the life-giving progenitor.

Scholars of religion have noted that sooner or later every primitive god becomes a bull. To the Egyptians, Apis, the sacred bull, was a reflection of the creator spirit. The bulls of Babylon were obviously symbols of divinity. The great, charging form of the bull-buffalo also became an emblem of the Great Mystery to those tribes whose very continued existence depended upon its flesh.

Grandmother Twylah of the Seneca has said that the buffalo represents force and strength. To dream of a buffalo is to receive a sign that you are being given support to accomplish a new endeavor. To envision the buffalo is to feel confidence in your ability to achieve your goals.

Should you have accepted the buffalo as your totem animal, you must play very close attention to the perception of important symbols that will manifest soon after the appearance of the buffalo in your dream. The careful analysis of these symbols will enable you to make an important decision or to solve a problem that has been nagging at you.

If the dream scenario has you being chased by an angry buffalo, you will soon receive a present.

If you stand your ground when the dream buffalo charges you, you will see a change in your luck for the better.

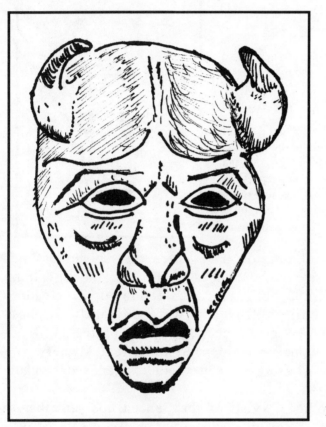

Cherokee
Buffalo mask.

Should you be surrounded by many buffalo, your guide is advising you that you are about to receive high honors. If those buffalo were especially plump and fat, you will enjoy a very fruitful year ahead of you. If they were a bit on the thin side, you will have to work hard, but you will succeed.

Butterfly Woman

BUTTERFLY The butterfly, a living fragment of a rainbow, floats with soundless wings above wild flowers on sunny currents of air. In the Dakota tradition, the butterfly represents the Door of the East, wherein appears the splendor of dawn in the dwelling place of the Great Mystery.

The butterfly denotes surrounding beauty, says Grandmother Twylah, and symbolizes people and conditions moving at a peaceful pace after a recent change.

In Christian sacred art, birds and butterflies depicted moving among foliage symbolize the souls of the blessed as they feed upon the pleasures in Paradise. Among the ancient Greeks, the word ps*yche* was used not only to denote the Soul, but was also the word for the butterfly, which came to symbolize the Soul.

If your dream guide has shown you a beautiful butterfly basking in the sunshine, you will be blessed with great happiness in love.

A dream in which a butterfly has entered your home may be an indication that you are about to experience some minor difficulties.

Should you have observed a lovely butterfly flitting from brightly colored flower to flower, you may expect to receive good fortune very soon.

The dream scenario that depicts you chasing after butterflies is warning you that certain individuals who are unfriendly toward you are doing their best to keep you from attaining your goal. Should you catch one of those butterflies, be alert to an act of unfaithfulness on the part of someone very close to you.

CAHOKIA MOUND If your guide has carried you in a dream to the remarkable Cahokia Mound near St. Louis, Missouri, spirit has a purpose in wanting you to be aware of the largest prehistoric earthwork thus far discovered in the United States. The mound's dimensions are 998 feet by 721 feet and 99 feet high. Archaeologists have also discovered over 45 mounds of smaller dimensions in the same area.

Go into the silence to learn what your association may be to this creation of the vanished Cahokia tribe.

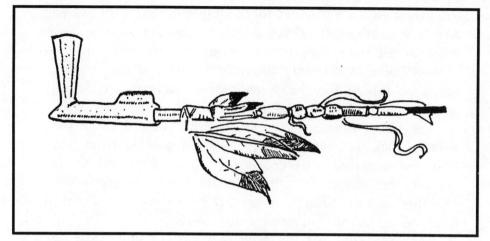

CALUMET The calumet (pipe) serves as the tool of blessing in so many traditional Medicine ceremonies. Stereotypically known as the "peace pipe," calumets were smoked in council--but to determine war, planting time, harvest, and social occasions, as well as peace. Smokes were used for tribal ceremonies, personal observations of sacred rituals, and for such diverse purposes as blessing the directions or summoning good spirits for important messages.

Strictly speaking, the calumet is the stem of the pipe, and it may be decorated or carved in an individual manner to denote particularly sacred occasions. Calumet is not an Indian word, but was likely derived from the Norman *chalumeau*, which indicated, in general, a pipe. Among the Iroquois, the sacred pipe was called *ganowdaoe*, and other eastern tribes referred to it as a *poagun*.

There are a number of quarries throughout the United States where the traditional Indians sought the stone especially prized for shaking their pipes. One of the most popular may still be seen near Pipestone, Minnesota.

As an old traditional story has it, many ages after the tribes of red men had been created, the Great Mystery was sad because so many of them were at war with one another. In an effort to accomplish peace, the Great Mystery sent spirit messengers to summon representatives of all the tribes to gather at the quarry of the red stone. There, transiently assuming human shape, he stood on top of the rocks in order to address all the red people assembled on the plain below.

The Great Mystery removed a piece of red stone from a large rock and fashioned from it a pipe. He filled the bowl with native tobacco, lighted it, and placed the stem to his mouth. Inhaling deeply, he drew the smoke into his mouth, then blew great, billowing clouds of it over all of those gathered below him.

"The red stone of the pipe is a part of your flesh," he told them. "Whenever evil thoughts of war enter your minds, you must sit down together and smoke a pipe of peace."

The Great Mystery instructed the red people that there should never be war at the quarry. Here, he commanded, all tribes must meet in peace. The quarry belonged to all of them, and they must make their pipes from its stone.

"You will blow clouds of smoke up to me whenever you seek my good will or wish to appease me," the Great Mystery said. "You will offer smoke to me whenever you desire messages of guidance."

With those admonitions completed, the Great Mystery blew great clouds of smoke over them all, and he disappeared in a swirling wind.

The Indians smoked *kinnikinnick*, a blend of various plants, including tobacco, sumac leaves, and the inner bark of the dogwood tree. *Kinnikinnick* is an Algonquin word meaning "mixed," and what was mixed for the Indians' pipe depended very much on what part of the country the tribe resided.

If your dream guide has shown you a night vision in which you are smoking the sacred calumet, you should soon realize the satisfaction of accomplishment. If you are the owner of several pipes, you will enjoy great peace of mind.

If the dream has made a point of the fact that you have permitted your pipe to become dirty, you will be liable to suffer through a time of misery and unhappiness.

A night vision that depicts you receiving a pipe as a gift has indicated that you will soon be promoted in your business or will achieve a particularly desired goal on your life path.

Should the dream have portrayed you as snuffing out the pipe and knocking the tobacco from the bowl, prepare yourself for the loss of a friend.

CHIEF Each tribe had many chiefs of varying grades and various responsibilities. There were specific titles given to chiefs for reasons that most often suited a particular expertise. While some tribes had a head chief, many, such as the Creek and the Iroquois had a complex parliamentary government. Some chiefs were awarded the title because of some remarkable act of courage. Few received the position due to hereditary lineage.

Scholars of the American Indian have rejected the Hollywood image of two men fighting over who would assume the position of chief in the village. The great chiefs of traditional times attained their spiritual power by a self-disciplined life of fasting, prayer, and a focus upon the needs of the village, not the individual.

The Medicine Priest Sun Bear once observed that among the plains Indians, a chief served only as long as he did the will of the people. If he got too stuck on himself, Sun Bear commented, "He'd go to sleep one night--and wake up the next morning to find that he was chief all by himself."

If you have dreamed of going to see a chief, you will probably receive good news and good fortune very soon.

If you have perceived yourself as a mighty chief, be alert to a painful deception in a love relationship.

If you, as the chief, saw yourself surrounded by many other chiefs and warriors, you may be about to be deceived by friends on whom you have counted for personal support.

A dream scenario which shows you killing a chief may foreshadow the death of a loved one.

COAT If you have dreamed of perceiving yourself in a new coat, quite likely you are about to be honored for some accomplishment.

If attention in a dream scenario was drawn to the tattered and frayed condition of an old coat that you were wearing, your guide is assuring you that prosperity is soon to arrive at your doorstep.

If you were shown wearing another person's coat in a dream, you will be forced to seek help from a friend. Should you trudge through a muddy area and get that coat dirty, you are in danger of losing a good friend.

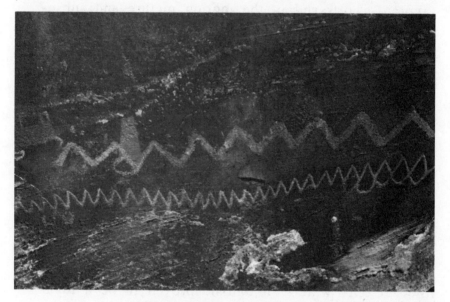

Bryce Canyon petroglyphs of the Serpent People.

CLIFF DWELLINGS If your guide has taken you on a night flight to visit a cliff dwelling, you should spend time in the silence to determine what your special connection to these places might be. There is no question that the dwellings project a most compelling, haunting quality; and if your dream becomes obsessive, you should travel to such ancient cities as Mesa Verde in Colorado or Montezuma Castle in Arizona. One cannot help admiring the skill of the ancient builders who crafted their homes on the sides of cliffs in natural rock shelters or caves.

To dream of being in such cliff dwellings with others may indicate a happy love relationship.

A dream of descending from a cliff may be warning you not to trust certain friends.

Standing high on top of a cliff, observing the dwellings below you, may caution you not to undertake any unnecessary risks in your business.

COCHISE This well-known chief of the Apache was favorably portrayed in the motion picture and subsequent television series, *Broken Arrow*, as a noble, spiritual warrior who sought only peace for his people. It was in 1861 that Cochise and a group of Apache chiefs went to an army post under a white flag of truce to explain to the officers that they had no part in the abduction of a white child. Tragically--and, unfortunately, typically--the commanding officer did not believe the chiefs and arrested all of them. Later, because they would not confess to the kidnapping, the officer ordered them all hanged. Cochise was the only one who escaped, even though he was wounded in his break to freedom.

Cochise entered a period of great despair when he realized that the ever-encroaching white man appeared to want only war. Although he proved to be a loyal friend to those settlers who wished to live in peace, Cochise organized the Apache and fought the "yellow legs," the U.S. troops, for ten years.

Defeated in 1871, Cochise died peacefully on June 8, 1874.

Arizona's Cochise County is named after this great chief of the Apache.

If you have felt the spirit of Cochise in your night visions or beheld an image you know to be his, you may be one who strives continually to be a diplomat in relationships and who wishes only harmony in human affairs. Go into the silence and seek to learn more about the reasons why you may be receiving guidance from Cochise.

COFFIN If you have dreamed of viewing a coffin designated as your own, be warned that someone close to you is attempting to cheat you. If you should have viewed yourself lying in state in that coffin, you are about to make a change in your life that will shower you with abundance.

Should you have viewed a room filled with coffins with no specific designation, your guide is advising you that you are accumulating unnecessary debts that can bring about your ruin.

A dream that depicts a close friend lying in a coffin is foreshadowing the approach of a serious illness to that person. If your friend's coffin is a particularly elaborate one, the dream may be warning of a possible death.

CORN Corn (maize) is one of the greatest of the food products bequeathed to the rest of the world by the American Indians. The versatile plant was to be found nowhere else on the planet, and it must be cultivated by human intervention or it cannot produce; consequently, corn constitutes one of the greatest of all mysteries offered by the Great Mystery.

Less than four decades ago, it was generally believed that human life did not exist in the Americas until about 5,000 years ago--and those early inhabitants were nothing more than primitive hunters. Then, in 1952, Dr. Paul Sears of Yale University dug up some maize pollen grains from about 240 feet below the surface of the dried lake bed on which Mexico City is built.

Maize (corn) is the most highly developed agricultural plant in the world--so highly developed that scientists have never been able to trace its original ancestors. According to radiocarbon testing, the pollen grains from the Mexican lake bed were at least 25,000 years old. Someone was harvesting domesticated maize in

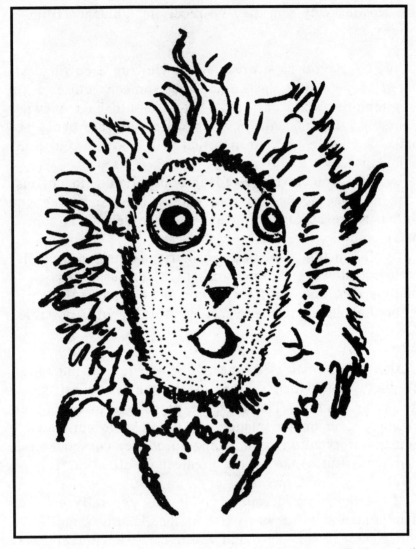

Iroquois corn husk mask

the Americas at least 20,000 years before anyone was supposed even to be smashing slow moving animals with clubs. Dr. Sears commented that anthropologists would now have to hunt for the ancestors of the Indians, as well as those of corn, much earlier than they had thought necessary.

The paradox of the great antiquity required to create corn, as opposed to the alleged time of human advent in the Americas was noted by the prominent botanist Daniel G. Brinton as early as the mid-1800s.

"...A lengthy course of cultivation is required so to alter the form of a plant that it can no longer be identified with the wild species; and still more protracted must be the artificial propagation for it to lose its power of independent life and to rely wholly on man to preserve it from extinction. Now this is precisely the condition of the maize, tobacco, cotton, quinoa, and mandioca plants....All have been cultivated from immemorial time by the aborigines of America, and except cotton, by no other race. All are no longer identified with any known wild species; several are sure to perish unless fostered by human care.

What numberless ages does this suggest? How many centuries elapsed ere man thought of cultivating Indian corn? How many more ere it spread over nearly a hundred degrees of latitude and lost all semblance to its original form? Who has the temerity to answer these questions?"

Thunder Spirit. The four rays emanating from the head represent fire. The mystic circle is held in one hand, an arrow in the other, thus indicating the spirit's ability to bring flaming arrows from the sky.

The Spirit of Vegetation. The spirit bears four rays of fire
on its head, signifying the warmth that is required to produce
green, growing things. The bow and arrow may represent an
aspect of the Thunder Spirit that is also a basic necessity to
vegetable growth, i.e., rain. The three lines radiating from the
right arm may indicate the sacred energy that flows from the
spirit to the earth to produce the sprig that it holds in its left
hand. The spirit seems to flow in decidedly feminine curves.

The spirit of the Corn Maiden was a symbol for the
bounty and the good will that the Earth Mother bestowed upon the Indian in a plentiful harvest of corn.
As Star-Spider Woman and Rattling Bear have observed,
"The Corn Maiden, the pubescent spirit, the virginal
goddess has latent within her all the potential of the
Earth Mother, the goddess of fertility."

If you have dreamed of fields of corn growing freely, you will be assured of plenty of money. The larger the ears on the cornstalks, the greater will be the amount of money headed your way. If there are no ears growing on the stalks, however, you are in for a great disappointment.

If you have seen yourself in a dream eating delicious corn on the cob, your guide is indicating that you will receive success in all of those present matters that have been troubling you so.

To dream of harvesting corn is a sign that you will soon be hearing some good news.

COUGAR Cougar, mountain lion, panther, and puma are all regional names for the same great tawny cat that once ranged throughout most of North America. To the Indian, the cougar was the lord of the hunt, the creature whose prowess in bringing down game was unsurpassed. "Now I am come up out of the ground,/I am ruler of the season" intones one chant in recognition of the cat's power on the trail.

A pictoglyph depicting the cougar as the mystic Lord of the Hunt. Its crescent ears represent the hunter's moon, and its long, exaggerated tail is capped with huge rattlesnake rattles. The parallelogram in the region of the heart indicates that the cougar has a heart of raging fire.

The cougar was imbued with many mystical qualities by the people of the various tribes. Its eyes resembled globes of fire at night or at dusk; its scream in the darkness could sound like that of a crazed female monster; and its method of quietly watching and slowly stalking its prey provided a model of caution and subtlety for the hunter.

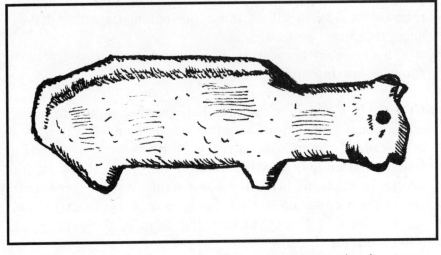

A stone carving representing the cougar.

The ancient Hebrews made use of the image of the eagle, the bull, and the lion as emblems of the Divine Being's power over air, fire, and light. An early missionary was reminded of this combination when ne witnessed an Indian ceremony which featured two white painted eagles with wings outstretched, a white clay figure of a man with buffalo horns, and the painted image of a cougar.

In many Mid-Eastern cultures the panther was considered a symbol of the "many-eyed Watcher," the unsleeping eye of the Divinity. In Egypt, the panther was representative of the Eye of Horus or of Osiris. An old superstition maintained that it was the sweet, fragrant breath of the panther that lured men, beasts, and cattle to their deaths under fang and claw.

Considered the Elder Brother by many American Indian tribes, worship or idealization of the cougar led

in certain areas to cults that believed they could transform themselves into the great cats by undergoing a
particular ceremony of transfiguration. Persistent rumors of such "cat people" made life in the early Ohio
valley uneasy for the white settlers who felt chills run
down their spines when they heard the terrifying night
call of the cougar.

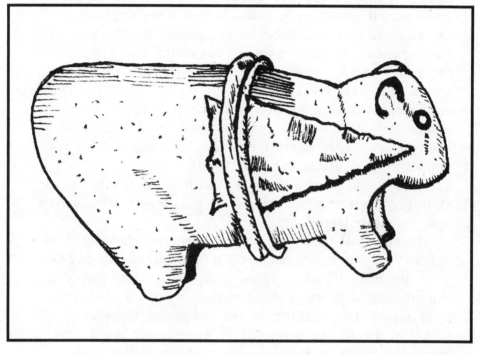

Zuni cougar fetish.

A dream in which you see a cougar at the mouth of its
lair is a medicine symbol that you will achieve victory over
your enemies. If the big cat attacked you and you escaped
unscathed, you will have continued successes on your
earthwalk. If you killed the panther, you will have to undergo a number of changes in your lifestyle before you may
achieve a final victory.

If your guide has sent you a dream in which you
heard cougars roaring in the distance, you were provided
with a symbol of approaching grief. If you walked
toward the roaring sounds and saw two cougars fight-

ing, you are being warned of a coming illness. If the cougars ran at your approach, the illness could become serious.

A dream drama in which you came across a dying cougar was advising you of the death of a person who plays a rather prominent role in your life.

If your night vision depicted you as surprising a cougar in the forest, you are being forewarned of the unsuspected deceit of friends. If you were frightened of the cougar, you will soon be persecuted by the acts of your enemies. If you regained your courage and chased the cougar away, you will be able to overcome the attacks of your rivals.

A dream drama that featured your coming upon a cougar in a cage was a sign from your guide that your enemies' activities against you may be curtailed by your maintaining a disciplined earthwalk.

If you saw yourself playing with cougar cubs in your night vision, you will soon be blessed with a new and valuable friendship.

If your visions or your quest have revealed the cougar as your totem animal, then its appearance in any of your dreams will be a signal from your guide that you should take note of a of important symbols that will soon follow the sighting of the cougar in the dream scenario. These symbols will be special messages sent from you guide to assist you in making difficult decisions and in solving problems that may have been vexing you. After you have taken note of them, you should analyze each one carefully in order to perceive the exact meaning of each symbol.

Opposite page:
Legends of a cult of cat people who attained the ability to transform themselves into cougars haunted many white frontier settlements. Certain statues recently unearthed give some credence to the worship of the cougar by various societies in many different tribes, especially in the Ohio valley.

COYOTE One of the tribes of old California believed that the coyotes were actually the first men who ever existed. In the beginning, they walked on all fours, then they began to grow certain human body parts--a finger here, a toe there, an ear here. Over the course of generations, they eventually became perfect humans--except for the loss of their tails, which gradually wore away through the process of sitting upright.

To another tribe, the coyote becomes an early, god-like savior of humankind. Originally, so goes the legend, the sun had nine brothers, all flaming hot like himself. Humankind was about to perish under such heat, but the coyote slew the sun's fiery brothers and thus saved the tribespeople from burning to ashes.

The coyote had no sooner dealt with the brothers of the sun than the moon's nine sisters, each as cold and icy as she, turned the night into a freezing torment. The coyote retreated to the far eastern edge of the world and made a fire with his knife of flint. After he had warmed his paws over the fire, he slew each of the moon's frigid sisters and saved humankind from freezing to death.

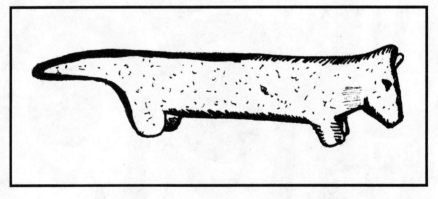

Zuni coyote fetish.

The coyote enjoys a most unique place in the legends and folklore of the North American Indian tribes. Although intimately associated with the Great Mystery in the act of creation, his wily descendants are both pests and competitors in the process of survival on the Earth Mother. It was the coyote who gave humankind the gift of fire, who taught the early people how to grind flour and showed them which herbs would bring about effective cures.

But one must always remember that the coyote has a very strange temperament. He is forever a Trickster, for although he brought fire into the world, he also brought death. When you ask such a creature to grant you the gift of a wish, you had better hope that you don't receive it--for there will be some twist attached to it.

Star-Spider woman and Rattling Bear have reminded us that being a creator, the trickster coyote has no conscience. "If fair means fail, he has no compunction using foul," they warn. "So if you must be foolish enough to ask [a favor], at least be precise in what you request."

If the coyote happens to be your totem animal, your guide is telling you to be alert to a series of important symbols that will appear in your dream after you have seen the coyote. These symbols will be integral in assisting you to solve problems that have been torment-ing you.

If you have dreamed of a coyote that stands alone on a hill, you may soon receive news of a death among your family or friends.

If you have seen yourself walking beside a coyote toward the darkness, be alert to trouble ahead.

A dream scenario in which you have injured a coyote tells you that you will soon receive an unexpected gift.

Should you dream of a coyote crossing your path as you are walking with a loved one, you would be well-advised to be on guard against that person's deceitful ways.

A dream in which you are making the coyote perform in an unnatural manner, such as dancing on its hind legs, is a warning that rumors are spreading about you.

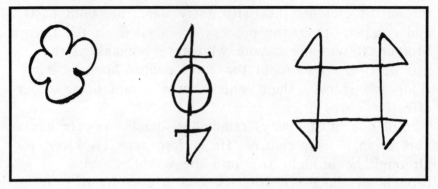

Glyphs representing the sacred number of four.

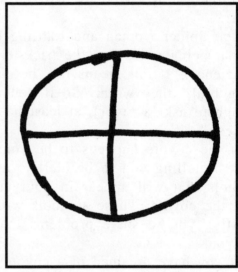

Earth and the four directions.

CROSS The cross represents the sacred number four in American Indian cosmology. There are the four directions, the four winds, the four cardinal points of the heavens.

A religious ritual that might represent a more or less typical employment of the sacred number four is expressed in a Mandan ceremony in which four sacks sewn of buffalo skin in the shape of a turtle were filled with water. The water therein symbolized the waters drawn from the four quarters of the world at the time of the "settling down of waters" at creation. Four shells were used by the Medicine Priest in the mystic dance. Four buffalo heads were placed within the Medicine tent. Four dancers clad in white, blue, black, and red represented the four spirits of the Earth Mother's dream.

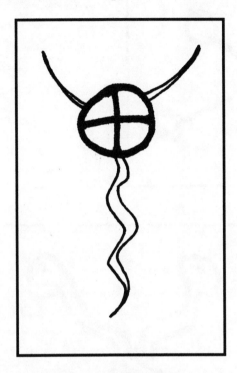

Glyph of the moon, the sun, and the four winds with the body of a serpent.

Grandmother Twylah, the Repositor of Seneca Wisdom, once delineated the power of the number four and the four-armed cross in this manner:

The first four creations were Sun, Moon, Water, Earth.

The four laws of creation are life, unity, equality, eternity.

The four seasons are spring, summer, fall, winter.

The four directions are east, north, west, south.

The four people of creation are white, red, yellow, black.

The four senses of feeling are seeing, hearing, tasting, smelling.

The four requirements of good health are food, sleep, cleanliness, good thoughts.

The four divisions of nature are spirit, mind, body, life.

The four divisions of goals are faith, love, work, pleasure.

The four ages of development are the learning age, the age of adoption, the age of improvement, the age of wisdom.

The four winds.

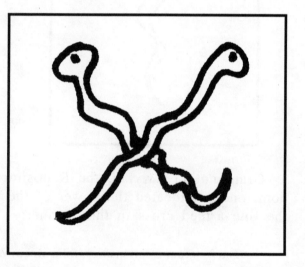

Crossed snakes
forming the sacred
number four.

To dream of the four-armed cross set apart by itself
is to receive a warning from spirit that trouble is on its
way.

If you have dreamed of a cross that appears somewhere on the flesh of your body, you should prepare
for emotional sorrow.

If you see yourself in the dream scenario wearing a
cross on your person, you are being informed that you
have the protection of spirit friends.

CRAZY HORSE This mighty chief of the Ogallala Sioux may have been the greatest of all mystic warriors. A closer translation of his name would probably have been "Horse That Will Not Be Tamed" or "Horse That Goes Its Own Way," either of which would mean a "crazy" horse to the white officers. Although no known photographs exist of this legendary chief, tradition describes him as a slender mystic, who relied completely upon the great power of his Medicine to lead his people successfully year after year.

When Crazy Horse took up the war ax against the whites, he allied his people with the Cheyenne to create a formidable fighting army. He is, of course, best remembered for his uniting with Sitting Bull for the great confrontation with General George Armstrong Custer at the Little Bighorn River on June 25, 1876. It was here that the United States Cavalry suffered its most smashing and well-publicized defeat at the hands of the Indians. Just a little less than a year later, Crazy Horse was defeated by U.S. Army artillery when the cannon unmercifully pounded his camps in the Bighorn Mountains.

The death of Crazy Horse is as shrouded in mystery as was his remarkable life. Placed under arrest on September 7, 1877, the official story has it that he was killed while trying to escape. Eye witness accounts of the Sioux present at his death denied such accounts and insisted that Crazy Horse was murdered. The site of his grave has never been discovered.

If your night visions have been receiving visitations from the spirit of Crazy Horse, you must seriously discipline your walk on the path of life to be able to absorb the full power and intensity of this great mystic. Go into the silence to learn how best to assimilate such spiritual power. Ask your guide to show you what your mission is to be--for if you are being touched by the spirit of Crazy Horse, there is no question that you have the responsibility of performing a great mission.

CROW This stately bird assumes a role in the traditions of the American Indian similar to its function in the legends of the old European tribes. Very often seen as a symbol of Death or Destiny, the crow was a messenger that was never ignored.

The Dakota envisioned the crow as an assistant to the Spirit of the South, who presided over warm weather. When the Spirit of the North came with his winter wolves, a battle was drawn between them and the crow and the plover, representing the Spirit of the South. If the crow and the plover were able to beat back the wolves with their warclubs, warm weather would prevail for a little while longer before the harsh cold set in over the plains.

If you have dreamed of a crow that seems only to sit on a branch of a tree and stare at you, you should prepare for disappointment to touch your life in every way. If the crow flies away at your approach, grief and misfortune are in the offing for you.

If your dream scenario depicts you as hearing the croaking sound of crows that remain unseen to your eyes, you are being warned of the approaching illness of children.

A dream of a large flock of crows flying overhead is liable to signal a death soon to occur in the family.

DANCE The traditional American Indian was a dancing person. All of the sacred rites, the preparation for the hunt and for war, the changing of the seasons--practically every aspect of village life was celebrated in song and dance. Many tribes performed ghost dances in the belief that the movement of the dancers and the beating of the drums could open a gateway to the world of spirits.

If you have viewed a traditional Indian dance in a dream, you will likely be granted success in love and in business.

If the dancers were clad in elaborate ceremonial garb, you may expect a windfall of prosperity.

A dream scenario which presented elaborately garbed traditional dancers moving with precision and grace was prepared by spirit to tell you not to worry about certain enterprises that have been causing you great concern. This scene was meant to show you that you will achieve success.

Should the dancers be moving gracefully before an audience of people with apparent illnesses, you have been presented with a sign that those loved ones who have been sick will make a change for the better.

If the ceremonial dancers were suddenly transformed into children, you will be given a great deal of joy in a happy home.

DEATH The American Indians had many rituals and practices concerning death and the dead. Black was the color of death and of mourning. A black circle signified the departure of the soul, whose journey was thought to be like that of the sun--a brief time beneath the great waters, then to rise again.

It was a general belief among most tribes that the world of spirit was similar to the physical world in its tasks and pursuits, hence the common reference to the "happy hunting ground," a place where all needs would be easily met.

There were Medicine priests among the Algonquin who taught that there were two souls residing in the physical body. One of the souls kept the body animate and remained with it during sleep. The other, less attached to the material plane, moved about at will, free to travel to faraway places and even to the spirit world. It was for the soul that remained with the physical body for which the Indians left food beside their dead.

The Dakota, among other tribes, believed that each person possessed four souls. One animated the body and required food; a second watched over the body, somewhat like a guardian spirit; a third hovered around the village; while the fourth went to the Land of Spirits at the time of physical death.

Certain of the eastern tribes told the legend of
Unkatahe, a serpent spirit that saw to the ushering of
souls from one plane of existence to another.

In the Chippewa cosmology, the soul passed to
another world immediately after death. Once in this
dimension of the afterlife, the soul would arrive at a
beautiful lake and be ferried across in a stone canoe. In
the middle of the lake was a magical island, and the
soul must wait in the stone canoe to await judgment for
its conduct during life. If its good actions predominated,
the soul would be permitted to reside on the magical
island. If the soul had spent a life seeking only carnal
and sensual gratification, the stone canoe would sink at
once and leave only the soul's head above the water.

Many tribes believed that spirits of the dead lingered among the living until certain rites had been performed to aid the spirits in their passage to the other
world.

Among the Ogallala, it was maintained that the
spirits of the dead passed into eternity by degrees at the
completion of necessary rituals that became the duty of
the deceased entities' families. Slowly, like fleeting
shadows, the spirits of the dead slowly migrated to the
other world, gaining strength for their journey from
the energy received from their living relatives as they
performed a long and demanding rite known as the
Shadow or Ghost Ceremony. As Ogallala lore recounts,
the time need to complete the ritual successfully could

amount to as long as two years, during which period the
immediate family and close relatives endured great pri-
vation to ensure the safe passage of the departed spirit.

These extensive rites were conducted in special lodges
that came to be known as Ghost Lodges. It was here
that the body of the deceased was kept prior to burial
and where the ceremonies on behalf of the departed
were continued long after his interment. The Ogallala
most often kept Ghost Lodges when the death was a
particularly sad one, such as the passing of a child by
accident or illness.

The Great Mystery in human form on this
pictoglyph [the figure on the right with the rays
emanating from the head] is depicted with the
ability to stop or start the human heart.

The duties of the Ghost Lodge most often fell upon the father or upon the nearest male relative and called for that individual to leave almost entirely the normal stream of village life in order to perform faithfully all the requirements of the ceremony that tradition demanded.

When a grieving family had made the decision to open a Ghost Lodge upon the death of a relative, criers were sent throughout the village to carry the message. A Medicine Priest was summoned so that the family might be guided in the more subtle intricacies of the sacred rituals.

The Medicine Priest was charged with taking the initial ceremonial steps of the Ghost Lodge, the smoking of a sacred pipe near the body of the deceased and the blowing of fragrant smoke to the four winds.

It was the sad duty of the father to dress the deceased in its finest clothing and to cut small locks of hair from the forehead for presentation to the mother. A large article of the departed one's clothing was cut into various lengths prescribed by the Medicine Priest, some to be buried in the Earth Mother, others to be consecrated to the buffalo, and the remaining pieces to be divided equally among the number of persons who had kept previous Ghost Lodges in the village. These strips, presented to prior lodge keepers, symbolized a silent appeal for help from the grieving father, an appeal that the Ogallala would never refuse.

The dancing society to which the deceased had belonged was called upon to conduct the death dances while the body lay in state inside the lodge.

The traditional burial ceremonies took place on the fourth day after death, but the real ordeal of the Ghost Lodge had just begun for the father of the deceased. It remained for him to complete a complex set of rituals that required him to spend the entire day inside the lodge, aiding the spirit on its trip to the other world.

A stringent set of taboos also went into effect by which both the grieving family and the other members of the village must conduct themselves. The nearest relatives of the deceased could eat no flesh scraped from the hide of any animal, and no weapon capable of shedding blood could be touched. It became the duty of other members of the village to hunt for the grieving family during the taboo period of the ghost vigil.

In the time when the family of the deceased was forced to rely upon others for their food, the mourners engaged themselves in the assembling of goods, which at the end of ceremony would be distributed as gifts to repay all the kind acts that had been done by their friends in their time of sorrow. Each member of the family worked daily to prepare countless beaded belts, headdresses, moccasins, strings of shell beads, and other items that would be given away by the family to mark the day when the spirit of their kinsman had passed into the arms of the Great Spirit and the doors to the Ghost Lodge were closed.

Strictly forbidden by the Ghost Lodge ceremony were any acts of a violent nature; and for fear of disturbing the air--and thereby the spirit of the deceased-- such prosaic deeds as running, swimming, or even shaking out a blanket were declared as taboo.

Perhaps most difficult of all, the father was not allowed to touch or to embrace any of his other children during the Ghost Lodge time, for fear that they might be harmed by whatever malevolent entity had claimed their kin.

To remind fellow villagers of the taboo in effect, the father kept to one corner of the family dwelling at night, separated from the others by a special fire that warned everyone not to approach him.

During the day, the father was required to spend his time in the Ghost Lodge with the spirit of the deceased. Food was brought to the lodge and set inside so the father could share a portion with the departing spirit.

Women were forbidden to approach the Ghost Lodge, and the men who entered to aid the father in his lonely vigil were required to follow a strict set of rules. For example, fires must be kept burning in the lodge, but they could not be blown upon to stir the flames. They could only be fanned with the wing of a bird. Although the medicine pipe could be smoked by the father, he was forbidden to share it with others--as was the normal custom--for fear that he might inadvertently offer the pipe to someone who had done violence, thus breaking the magic needed to complete his sorrowful duties.

The cost to the family could be staggering. The father may be expected to present gifts of ponies and weapons to the Medicine Priests and to other friends who had been of special assistance, but a man who had successfully conducted a Ghost Lodge was known to the rest of the village as one who did not shirk his duties and as one who could be trusted with high office in the conduct of tribal affairs. When a man of the Ogallala had completed his time as the keeper of a Ghost Lodge, he was a man to be held in esteem. He had undergone an almost superhuman regimen to shepherd the spirit of his kin safely to the world of the grandfathers.

The keeper of the Ghost Lodge who had completed his obligations to his kin knew also that when his day came, there would be others who would take the lock of hair from his head and sing the ancient chants before the straw pallet upon which he lay in the great and final sleep. And for the devout Ogallala who wished above all things to spend his eternity with the Great Mystery, that was a very comforting thing to know.

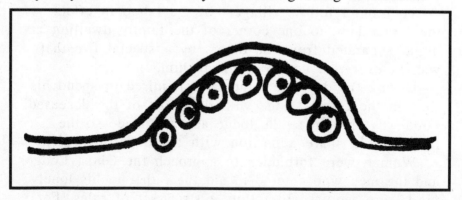

The circles and the curved lines are representations of the spirits of the stars and the sky.

There were also tribes who believed that their eternal abode would be in the stars. To these people, the Milky Way was known as The Pathway of the Dead; and it was their custom to light fires upon the graves of the dead for four days to give them ample time to arrive safely in the heavens, on the glorious island.

Ambrose Bierce's rather morose observation that in the midst of life we are all in death was echoed by such Medicine Priests as the Winnebago shaman who, sorrowing for the loss of a loved one, drew lines upon sandy soil, then uttered the following words: "We are all like these lines. Today we are here and can be seen. But death will take away one...then another...just as the wind removes lines in the sand until all are gone."

Then, stooping above the lines that he had etched in the soil, he obliterated all of them with quick movements of his hand. "They are all gone now--and like them we shall vanish and shall be seen no more."

Before leaving to grieve in private, the Medicine Priest spoke softly, "Grieve not, our brother, for the path that thou art walking is that on which we and all men must follow."

It seems likely that all Medicine Priests believed that the spirits of the dead could be recalled by the aid of powerful Medicine rituals, charms, and ceremonial dances. And it is one of the basic tenets of Medicine Power that the dead may transmit messages to the living during the dream state.

If you have experienced a dream in which you spoke with a dead friend, you may expect a change for the better in your personal affairs. If you spoke with a deceased relative, you will soon be contacted by a living relative.

Should your dream scenario have portrayed you, the dreamer, as dying, you were being given a sign that happiness and good fortune are in store for you.

If you viewed the death of a pregnant woman, you will receive good news from a faraway source.

Should you have witnessed the death of a young girl or
boy in your dream, you will soon experience a pleasant
family event.

To have a dream in which you come upon the corpse
of a relative is to have been given a sign that your love
relationship will turn sour and unhappy.

If you have viewed several corpses in your night
vision, you may be in peril of death. You should become extremely cautious until you sense the danger has
passed.

Should your dream scenario reveal your own grave,
interpret this as a sign that your enemies are plotting to
bring disaster to you.

If you yourself are digging a grave, you will face
very big obstacles in overcoming the plans of your
enemies.

An integral part of initiation for many shamans is a
state of pseudodeath that comes upon one in illness or in
trance and during which one appears literally to have
died. Traditionally, the shaman remains dead for three
days, then, in effect, rises from his grave and continues
his life very much changed. He has now been to the
spirit world. His soul has soared to other worlds and
dimensions of time and space. He has come back from
the dead to tell his people that there is no death, only a
change of worlds.

If you have dreamed of watching someone come back
to life after death, you will receive a high honor from
your peers. If you have envisioned your own death and
your return to life, you are about to undergo a revela-
tory experience that will bring you much peace and
enlightenment.

The Strange Death Dreams of Morning Song

Many a cold winter evening in the rugged uplands of Montana has been warmed by the story of the dreams of Morning Song and her great love for her husband, Two Bears.

It was in the early winter days of 1878 that the two white trappers Ben Suttler and Jim Martin spotted the slim and beautiful young Crow woman leading a gaunt pony up the rocky hillside that led to their wilderness camp. The harsh moon of cold and snow would soon grip the Montana uplands, and it was no time for a young woman to be making her way higher into the purple mountains where the snow already lay heavily.

"She must think that she's got some all-powerful business to be making her way up to the big snow country," Martin said over the edge of his tin mug. "Go on and signal her for some of this mountain tea and some grub to warm her innards, and maybe we can find out what is so all-fired important to the girl."

Morning Song was cautious of the large, bearded white man who hailed her from the camp set back in a clump of trees, but she soon recognized Ben Suttler as one who had visited her village many times with trade goods. Half-frozen, she graciously accepted their hospitality.

After several steaming cups of the mountain men's herbal tea, Morning Song told them that she was traveling in search of her husband, Two Bears: "Many days ago he left on a hunting trip to lay up food for the time of the cold moons and the snow, and he has not returned. I know that he needs my help."

The trappers questioned her further, wanting to know why she felt thus so convicted that she would venture out into the frost-covered wilderness.

"Two Bears came to me in a dream," Morning Song said earnestly. "He told me that he lies wounded in the foothills. He asked me to come to his aid. He needs my help to return to our village."

Martin and Suttler exchanged meaningful glances. They had seen too many convincing examples of Indian Medicine power to doubt the truth of her dream, but they also feared for the young woman's safety in the hostile wilderness.

"Old Thunder Moon is the Medicine man in your village," Martin reminded her. "What did he have to say about all this?"

Morning Song looked downcast into the dwindling flames of the campfire. After Two Bears had been gone for nine days, she told the trappers, Thunder Moon had said that she should accept the reality that her husband had been killed by a bear or a war party of Blackfeet.

"Thunder Moon told me to put on the clothes of mourning and to cut my hair and to wail as a woman whose man is no more," Morning Song said bitterly. "I have always been an obedient daughter and wife, but I refused to do as Thunder Moon bade me. I told him that I know that Two Bears is alive. His spirit has come to me in a dream, and I must go to him somewhere in the hills where he waits for me to help him."

The young wife told the two mountain men that even though the Crow elders believed that her dream was one born only of grief, they did not attempt to stop her as she left the camp leading the small pony upon whose back she had packed herbs with which to heal her husband.

Jim Martin and Ben Suttler were moved by the strength of Morning Song's love and by the power of the dream that had brought her over many dangerous miles in search of her husband. While they had not encountered Two Bears in their own forays across the mountains, they thought it possible that some news of his whereabouts might be found in a Blackfoot village not far from their trap lines. The village was a large one that sprawled at the crossroads of several trade routes, and news of any wilderness event sooner or later found its way there.

When the two mountain men took Morning Song to the village, the Blackfeet put aside the animosity born of many generations of conflict with her tribe and invited the beautiful and brave woman to remain with them and await whatever word might reach them about the fate of Two Bears. Martin and Suttler presented her story to Chief Crooked Arm, and the account of her loyalty to her husband brought her respect in his eyes. He ordered his people to treat Morning Song with honor, and he saw to it that she was provided with a comfortable lodge in which wise women might visit her and seek to calm her anxiety.

While in the Blackfoot camp, Morning Song continued to experience her dreams of Two Bears. The night visions became even more vivid, and finally, on one night, Two Bears said, "My faithful one, you must come to me, for my hour is near. My wounds are great and need your healing hands."

Spurred by the urgency of the dream and the anguish in the words of Two Bears, Morning Song prepared to leave the Blackfoot camp and to set out again in search of her husband. She grieved that she had rested those few days in the village while her husband lay injured and untended.

As Morning Song was leading her pony from the lodge in which she had been given hospitality, a brave from a nearby Blackfoot encampment rode into the village astride a pinto pony that she knew belong to Two Bears. "Why is it that you ride upon my husband's horse?" she demanded of the startled Blackfoot brave.

Though he had first refused to reply to the Crow woman, whom he assumed must be a captive, Crooked Hand ordered him to explain at once where he had found the horse and what had happened to its owner.

The young warrior told a story that was very familiar in those days of rivalry between the tribes that lived side by side along the Montana ranges. Two Bears had been surprised by a Blackfoot hunting party and had been badly wounded by a tomahawk blow. He had been taken captive to the Blackfoot camp, and he had lain in a lodge for two weeks, calling out for his wife before he at last died of his wounds.

Morning Song felt the brave's words pierce her heart as if they were cruel war arrows. Two Bears was dead. And he had died calling her name.

Yes, the Blackfoot brave said. He had called the name of Morning Song many times while he lay dying. Those who watched him heard him beseech his wife to come to his side.

Morning Song permitted no tears of sorrow to escape from her eyes. She was in the camp of her tribal enemy, and she would show them that Crow women did not weaken, even in the face of death.

But Morning Song said a strange thing to the Blackfoot who had brought the sad news, and all those who had pressed forward to hear the account wondered at her words. "When you return to your camp, tell Two Bears that I am coming. Tell Two Bears that I will join him soon."

The young brave wheeled on the pinto and left the uncomfortable scene with haste. The woman was the wife of the enemy that they had killed. He could comprehend if she had screamed and cursed him. Her quiet resolve made him feel uneasy.

It soon became apparent to the women in the Blackfoot village what Morning Song had meant by her strange words. She refused to eat, and she told the concerned women who came to her with food that it would be only a few days before she would join Two Bears, just as he had pleaded in her dream.

The elders among the Blackfoot women tried to persuade Morning Song that nothing could be gained by her death. She was a beautiful young women whom many of the braves in the village admired for her courage and her loyalty. She could lead a long and happy life if she would but stay among her new friends.

But Morning Song could not be dissuaded, and as she had foretold, the white horse of death came within a few days to take her to the place of spirits where Two Bears waited.

The Blackfoot people mourned the proud young woman of the Crow who had died with such courage. To honor her, Morning Song's body was carried to the place where Two Bears had been buried, and the two were placed side by side. It was as the dream had foretold: She had come to join Two Bears forever.

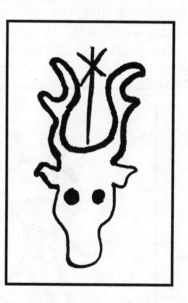

In addition to the American Indian's well-known respect for the deer, many cultures represented the antlered stag as the symbol of the Perfect and Eternal Spirit.

DEER If the deer is your totem animal, your guidance is alerting you to watch for a number of important symbols which will appear after you have sighted the deer in your dream. These symbols may appear overtly or be subtly woven into the context of your dream scenario, but they have been placed within the night vision to assist you in making an important decision or to direct you to a better path in order to solve problems that have been disrupting to your mission in life.

If you have dreamed of a deer bounding through the forest, you will soon receive good news. If you perceived several deer in motion, there will be money along with the good news.

To dream of a solitary deer that keeps jumping just ahead of you, constantly eluding you, is to receive a symbol of troubles lying ahead.If your dream placed you among a herd of deer, you may be assured of having many good friends. If the herd runs from you, you should be wary of approaching financial distress.

If you have viewed yourself killing a deer while on a hunt, you will receive an inheritance. If you have only the antlers of a deer to show for a hunt, the dream is informing you that you will be cheated by friends or business associates. To dream of eating the meat of a male deer after a successful hunt is to receive a sign that you will survive difficult times ahead.

The Delaware and the Chippewa
tribes saw in this pictoglyph the evil snake
spirit that seeks to destroy humans.

DEVIL Until the advent of the Christian missionaries, it would probably be correct to state that, in general, the Indian's concept of evil spirits was somewhat different from that of most other theologies. Most Medicine Priests perceived the lower entities to be more mischievous than destructive and considered that each spirit had the capacity for both good and for evil.

There were, of course, those spirits who chose to be evil and to afflict the human body with diseases and various other torments of the flesh. The machinations of such entities were to be dreaded and exorcised by the Medicine Priest whenever and wherever possible. There was, however, no personal Devil whose express purpose was to lead humankind into hellish snares of damnation.

Certain tribes did personify the Evil One in one body, a bizarre amalgamation of the most disagreeable

Many tribal legends tell of the time when the heroes of old were forced to fight the enemy snake beings for their survival as a species.

aspects of many animals. The entity had two feet shaped
like the panthers, scales like the alligator, the tail of a
black snake, the broad shoulders of the buffalo, the
eyes of the lobster, the beak of a vulture, topped off
with ivory teeth in its jaws, and porcupine quills on its
head. The Indians believed that such a creation was a
mistake committed by the Great Mystery, and in no
way did they understand that such a misshapen monster
sought to tempt humankind or to lead it from the path
of spiritual evolution.

In one common Indian legend of the struggle between
Good and Evil, the Great Mystery creates the two op-
posing forces as brothers. Brother Good goes forth to
create all beautiful and pleasant things, while Brother
Evil seeks to thwart such efforts by making hard and
flinty places and causing bad fruits to grow. And just as
Brother Evil seeks tirelessly to work mischief, Brother
Good ceaselessly strives to repair the results of his

Delaware
representation of the
Bad Spirit that
commands snakes,
monsters, and giant
reptiles.

troublesome sibling. When Good at last wearies of his brother's mischief, he challenges him to a race in which the winner gets to chose where the loser shall live. Good triumphs and sends Evil away to the icy, frozen north to reside. A sore loser, Evil slinks off with the threat that all who follow him shall die and never return from the Land of Eternal Silence.

Students of religion will be reminded of the Hindu tradition that unites the destructive and reproductive principles in the deity of Shiva, or the benevolent and destructive twin-brothers Osiris and Typho, gods of

Pictoglyph of an evil priest.

ancient Egypt. In Persian mythology, to cite only one more example, the beneficent Ormuzd and his brother Arimanes, the prince of darkness, are the product of the one supreme essence.

It is interesting to note that the faraway north country has the same sinister and evil reputation among many other cultures. Arimanes, Persian mythology's prince of darkness, resides in the north. Milton, in his epic poem of creation, *Paradise Lost*, enthrones Satan "high on a hill" in "the limits of the north."

The witchcraft laws of the Apache comprised a stern code, containing a complex set of procedural rules. When Sacred Priests found evidence of those within the tribe who were using malevolent powers to harm others for revenge or for gain, they immediately brought the malefactor to trial.

The Apache believed that witches could exercise their evil powers in many ways, but if one were observant and watched the suspects carefully, they would betray themselves through the use of several favorite methods for casting spells.

Apache witches were known to knead lumps of clay and to form small likenesses of their victims on which they might inflict the symbolic injury that they wished their unfortunate prey to experience in reality. Such a practice is very closely akin to the rites of Voodoo practiced in the Caribbean where dolls are used in the process of casting a spell upon a victim.

The use of the so-called "evil eye" was another method by which witches might gain control over their prey. In times when accusations of witchcraft were being made, members of the tribe would avoid one another's gaze in order to keep them aloof from unfounded accusations.

The familiar spirit most often employed by Apache sorcerers was the owl. Although the bear was used in rare instances, the powerful animal was more often associated with the powers of light; and the Apaches left the bear unmolested, except in self-defense. Because the bear was often seen to be walking erect on its hind legs, the Apache--and most other tribes, as well-- believed the creature to be somehow related to humans, and, therefore, sacred.

A hex sign. The crossed lines obliterate the figure's face, thereby suggesting the act of destroying an enemy. The chant accompanying this figure reads, "I have caused this one to look like a dead man."

Charges of witchcraft, perhaps the most serious of any Apache crime, were brought with great caution only after the suspect had been carefully watched for many days. Because malevolent witchcraft was one of the very few tribal infractions that demanded the pen- alty of death, the evidence that had been collected against the accused had to remain in the minds of the accusers as irrefutable.

If such clear and unquestioned evidence was brought to the chief, a jury was selected, and a trial on the charge of witchcraft was held. Any tribal member known to have been guilty of lying in the past was barred from testifying against the accused. There would be no one bearing false witness and telling lies to bring death to a rival.

Most often the accusation would be made by the person who believed himself to be suffering under the witch's spell--or by the family of a victim who had died from what was believed to have been the witch's curse.

Tests of logic were always required during the trial: Had the accused and the victim ever quarreled over horses, women, or trade goods? Was there some way in which the accused stood to profit if death befell the victim? Such were the questions that an Apache jury weighed before rendering a final verdict.

In those cases wherein the awful charge was considered proved, the decree of death that followed oftentimes did not issue directly from the jury, who may have been contented with ordering banishment from the tribe. Most often the death sentence was carried out by relatives or friends of the witch's victim, who would trail the evil one secretly away from camp and take the ancient revenge of spilling blood.

To the Apache, few crimes were deemed more serious than that of converting to evil the forces that the Great Mystery had put into the world for good. When death was pronounced upon the head of an Apache witch, the decree came only after a soul-searching examination by the persons who had brought the charges--and only after their allegations had been painstakingly demonstrated and proved in a court convened to find the truth.

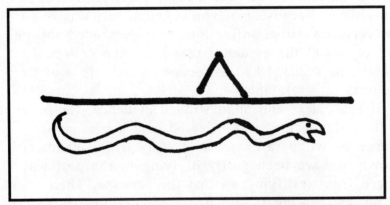

Pictoglyph of the Evil One Who
Lives Under the Ground.

If you have dreamt of a personification of evil represented by a demon or a devil, your guide unquestionably
has something important to tell you about your life
path--and it will behoove you to pay close attention to
an analysis of your dream symbols relating to this
matter.

The dream image of a devil with overly large horns
and an extremely long tail may be warning you of a
misfortune in a love relationship.

If the dream scenario has depicted you engaged in a
lengthy conversation with the devil, you are probably
being cheated by friends whom you have trusted.

Wa-hun-de-dan, Dakota
spirit of war and strife.

Should you attack the devil and engage him in a physical fight, you are in a great deal of danger. If, however, you injure or wound the devil, you will escape a trap set for you. Should you persist in the fight and conquer him, you will triumph over your enemies.

A dream in which you see yourself being carried off by the devil foreshadows a serious personal disaster ahead. A night vision which portrays you being chased by the devil and running away indicates a legal battle in your future.

Should your night vision depict you entering a home possessed by evil spirits, be exceedingly careful in business matters for the next several days.

If your dream displays evil spirits causing sorrow to yourself or to your close family members, be wary of friends who are plotting to cheat you.

DOG The dog, in Grandmother Twylah's view, represents fidelity and devotion. The dog symbolizes a friend who is always available when he or she is truly needed.

The Osage tell a story that not only illustrates the loyalty and faithfulness of dogs toward their human companions, but also demonstrates the intense bonding that can occur between the four-leggeds and the two-leggeds. This tale begins some time around 1889 in Oklahoma Territory, just before the big land rush by the whites to grab up their chunks of the Earth Mother.

It seems that Roaring Thunder, a young Osage brave, became suddenly ill and appeared to die. When it seemed that he had stopping breathing, his kinsmen quickly did the traditionally sensible thing and buried him.

But it was Roaring Thunder's dogs who were the wise ones. Chinka and Mowta, his faithful mongrels, knew that the spark of life still burned within him. They knew that their master's two-legged brothers had buried him, unwittingly, alive.

Chinka and Mowta pawed away the shallow covering of earth under which the villagers had lain Roaring Thunder and used their strong teeth to grasp the burial

robe and to pull him from the grave. It was their nudging and nuzzling that had brought him back to consciousness and led him on a sorrowful journey back from the dead.

When Twin Feathers, the aged widow of Big Wolf, saw Roaring Thunder walking in his burial robe toward Tall Chief's camp in the first light of dawn, she began to scream. Only two days before, she had helped to place Roaring Thunder into the arms of the Earth Mother.

The rest of the village agreed with Twin Feather's fear. In spite of Roaring Thunder's assurances that he was not dead, that he had only fallen into some strange kind of sleep in his sickness, his kinsmen had no doubt that he was a ghost and that he had returned to wreak some terrible vengeance on someone who had done him some wrong in life.

Although he had been well-liked in the village, Roaring Thunder now found every tepee closed to him. From behind tightly fastened door flaps, he heard every member of his family shout at him to go away. According to them, he was a malevolent spirit come to work evil on the village. He only pretended to speak with Roaring Thunder's voice and to act like him.

No amount of tearful entreaty could convince the Tall Chief band of the Osage that Roaring Thunder had not truly died, but had only fallen into a deep sleep from which he had awakened. At last, with a broken heart, the young man accepted the cruel judgment that his tribe had placed upon him. His heart swelled with even greater love for his dogs, Chinka and Mowta, who had proved their loyalty when all others had run from him in fear. They would be his only friends now--and for all the years that lay ahead.

Although he tried from time to time to return to his village and to explain that his escape from the grave was not due to evil spirits, Roaring Thunder finally ceased trying to gain re-acceptance among his own people; and he became a lonely wanderer across Oklahoma territory, striding the plains and the hills with his faithful dogs foraging ahead.

There were some white settlers in the area who were acquainted with comas and the tragedy of premature burial and could understand what had happened to Roaring Thunder. They also wished to help the outcast Osage and to be his friends.

Oklahoma had become a state in 1907, and Roaring Thunder's sympathetic white friends assisted him to file a claim for a small piece of land to which he was entitled under certain old treaty provisions. Chinka and Mowta had left him for the good hunting in the spirit world, but their three pups were there--along with four or five other mongrels--so Roaring Thunder set about pitching a semi-permanent camp on his treaty land.

And then the Great Spirit smiled on Roaring Thunder in a manner that was almost incomprehensible to the outcast. He had heard strange stories about crazy white men who searched for "black gold" in the hard Oklahoma earth. When he permitted some of the *loco hombres* to dig where he and his dogs made their home, great geysers of the dark, ugly, useless oily water spurted skyward. Soon, for reasons that he was never quite able to grasp, Roaring Thunder was a rich man with powerful medicine in the white man's banks.

Friendly guardians appointed to watch over his new wealth built Roaring Thunder a fine log house near the boomtown of Pawhuska; and for a time the Osage wanderer was persuaded to sleep inside its comfortable walls.

But his dogs did not take to the rules and regulations of life in the white man's village, and Roaring Thunder sensed the untamed spirits of his old friends Chinka and Mowta in the restless pacing of their descendants. He made an excuse about needing to go out for cigars, and he fled with his faithful dogs to the open plains and hills that had sheltered them when he was considered an outcast.

For years thereafter, concerned friends watched the Oklahoma hills for signs of the old man and his loyal dogs. From time to time, settlers would set out caches of supplies in places that they knew Roaring Thunder would frequent in his long walks across the plains. Sometimes a few things would be taken--most often the big cigars that he so enjoyed--but the wanderer pre- ferred to live by his keen hunting skills and to take from the Earth Mother no more than what was needed by an old man and his dogs.

In 1938, Roaring Thunder fell among the rocks of the rugged hills that he loved. For six months, he lingered with a broken limb that the white Medicine man told him would not heal. Confirming the doctor's decree with his own inner-knowing that he would never again be able to walk the Oklahoma plains and hills, Roaring Thunder slipped quietly into the great sleep of death that he had cheated so many years before.

His beloved four-legged friends followed the coffin to the place near Pawhuska where the old warrior was buried; and as the dogs kept watch over Roaring Thunder's grave, the mournful notes of their sad howl- ing blended into a death song that carried him to the sides of Chinka and Mowta, the two inseparable com- panions of his youth.

If you should happen to dream of a sad dog, Grand- mother Twylah warns you that such a symbol repre- sents someone with a lack of self-understanding. Such an individual waits for others to handle his problems because he has lost his own initiative. People with such a trait are martyrs looking for sympathy. They should be avoided, Grandmother admonishes, because they are "energy-drainers."

To dream of a pet dog is to receive a symbol of hap- piness.

If you have dreamed of a large dog that belongs to another, you are being shown that you have many friends. If that dog performs an act of courage, you are being told that your friends are loyal to you.

Should you dream of a dog with a shaggy coat, the symbol is informing you that your lover is truthful and may be trusted. A barking dog warns you that you and your lover are about to quarrel.

If your dream scenario has displayed a scene of dogs fighting one another, guard your home against a break-in by thieves.

If you have perceived yourself being chased by a dog, be aware that others seek to ruin your reputation. If the dog tears your clothes, the gossip comes from among your own family members. If the pursuing dog turns and bites someone other than you, the destructive gossip originates from within your circle of friends. If the dog bites you, be wary concerning your being double-crossed by someone you have considered a close friend.

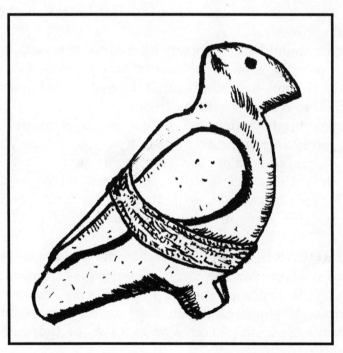

Zuni eagle fetish.

EAGLE Because the eagle could fly so close to the sun, the large bird was regarded as a special messenger to and from the Great Mystery. In the old days, eagle feathers were used on war bonnets, rattles, shields, pipes, baskets, prayer sticks, and ceremonial costumes. The very manner in which the eagle feathers were clipped, colored, and arranged on a chief's or warrior's clothing could reveal his rank in the tribe and the types of deeds which he had accomplished.

If the eagle has been revealed to you as your totem animal, its appearance within your dreams will signal the approach of important symbols that your guidance has sent in order to assist you with the solution of problems and troubles that have been causing you stress and concern. Pay close attention to the symbols that follow the manifestation of an eagle in your dreams.

To dream of watching an eagle flying high above you is to be advised of good fortune ahead.

Should that eagle swoop downward to earth and attack you, you may expect many difficulties in the days that lie ahead.

If you should have dreamt of finding a wounded eagle, you may soon experience a loss in your love relationship. If you have discovered a dead eagle, you will be liable to suffer financial losses.

If your night vision has shown you a magnificent eagle perched high on a mountaintop, you are on your way to receiving fame and fortune. If that high-flying eagle should descend to sit upon your shoulder or upon your extended arm, you will also receive many honors and extensive recognition in your field.

EARTHQUAKE If your guide has presented you with a dream in which you have felt an earthquake, you may have experienced a presentiment concerning the death of a relative. If you dreamt you were in the vicinity of an earthquake, you may soon receive news of the transition of a close friend.

Should you have viewed the destruction of a city by earthquake, your dream is advising you of a great change that is about to take place in your life.

Feathers were used as common accoutrements to dress and as emblems symbolizing the flight of the spirit through the air. Because of the birds' ability to fly upward toward the sun, the celestial orb itself was believed to be their ruler.

FEATHER Grandmother Twylah of the Seneca says that a feather represents good news. When the feather has no openings in its plume, the news is welcome and it comes all at once. When the feather is separated with holes, the news will come in intervals. The feather also symbolizes strength, support, and good will from others.

To envision yourself wearing tufts of feathers is to have a dream foretelling great honors coming to you.

If you have seen yourself in a dream scenario collecting multicolored feathers, you have received a foreshadowing of receiving joy throughout your life.

FIRE As might be expected, fire, with its life-preserving qualities, was regarded by the Indians as sacred. To many shamans, fire had been brought to the Earth Mother by a serpent as a symbol for the source of all life. Many Medicine Priests viewed fire as a kind of connecting link between the natural and the supernatural worlds and that spirits could dwell within the dancing flames.

Most tribes referred to fire as if it were an active,

intelligent being. A Shawnee Medicine Priest once observed to his people that the life in their bodies and the fire on their hearths are one and the same thing--and that both proceed from the same source.

Certain sacred fires were kept burning continually for religious rites, their embers fanned to life by the wings of a white bird.

The Cherokee waved a child's body over fire immediately after its birth, and their hunters held their moccasins over flames to protect them against rattlesnake bites.

If you have dreamed of poking up the flames in your fireplace, your guide may be warning you to assume better control over your temper.

Should you dream of a blazing fire of large proportions, you will soon receive a great deal of happiness.

A dream of fire falling from the sky is sent to warn you of possible destruction of prized possessions.

A dream scenario in which you reach for an object in the midst of flames with your bare hand and do not suffer burns is assuring you that you will achieve the goals you seek.

If you have dreamed of someone falling into a fire, your guide is foreshadowing a coming misfortune. If you see a relative on fire, you may soon be running a fever. If you yourself suffer burns in a fire, you have seen a symbol of your business being seriously damaged.

FISH Fish constituted one of the basic food items for many tribes. As a universal symbol, the fish is revered by many cultures. One thinks immediately of the early Christians who adopted the sign of the fish as a symbol of Christ. The fish was sacred among the Babylonians, Phoenicians, and Assyrians and was esteemed as an emblem of fertility. To many primitive people, the fish serves as a symbol of knowledge, for it dives deeply to explore the unknown depths of the waters. According to the most ancient of traditions, instructions in all fields of endeavor were provided by a fishlike being to the priests in Sumer, the cradle of civilization.

Grandmother Twylah of the Seneca advises that a brightly colored fish, arrayed in all its glory, may represent a disappointment in a forthcoming gala event. The "frills" in life, Grandmother reminds us, may not always provide a good experience.

If your dream drama has depicted you leaning over a clear stream observing a number of fish swimming freely about, you may expect to hear news of good fortune. If you perceived dead fish floating on the surface of the stream, expect to learn of a troublesome situation.

If you have dreamt of catching some fish, you will soon learn how much you are loved. If you are watching fish moving about in shallow water and you seem unable to catch them, you should be on guard against a serious loss of reputation.

A dream in which you are on a fishing trip with relatives may be warning you to be on guard against harmful gossip. A fishing trip with a close friend may be suggesting that you are spending too much time enjoying expensive pleasures. If you and your friend pull in some large fishes, you will earn ample money to support your desires. If the fish are small, you will suffer financial reverses.

FLOWER To dream of many blooming flowers is to have assurance from your guide that you will experience pleasures in your future.

A young woman who dreams of walking among many beautiful flowers will have many earnest suitors after her hand in marriage.

If either a young woman or man is shown a dream scenario in which the picking of flowers seems to be the principal activity, there is a marriage on the horizon.

A field of red flowers perceived in a dream often presages death for the dreamer or for a loved one.

If your dream has you throwing away a bouquet of

flowers, you may expect a violent quarrel with a family member.

A dream in which you receive a gift of flowers from a faraway source is probably indicating the exciting news that you have just become heir to a fortune.

A flower, according to Grandmother Twylah, represents the artistic dimension of creativity. The bud of a flower is a symbol of new ideas about to spring into existence.

FLUTE In the traditions of certain Southwestern tribes, the very act of creation was piped into existence by two mute men who gave life to all things through the magic of their flutes.

If you dream of playing the flute to the approval of your audience, you may expect money to come easily to you for the rest of your life. If, in your night vision, you are only listening to others play the flute, you may anticipate difficulties in the acquisition of funds to continue to plague you. If your dream featured a young child or many children playing flutes, you will probably receive news of the birth of a child to a friend or family member.

FOX In the traditions of many tribes, the fox is often associated with witchcraft, and it may even serve as the image of transformation for a sorcerer or witch, the practitioner of negative Medicine Power. In Europe, the fox was the symbol of wiliness, quick-wittedness, and a kind of crafty wisdom.

If the fox has revealed itself to you as your totem animal, then its appearance in your dream vision will signal you to be on the alert for a series of important symbols that will follow its manifestation in the dream scenario. A thoughtful analysis of these symbols will assist you in making important decisions or in solving vexing problems assailing your life path.

In most dream visions, the fox will represent an enemy or a rival who hides himself among your acquaintances as an individual friendly toward you. If you should dream of killing a fox, your guide has indicated that you will overcome any threat of trouble instituted by the deceit of this enemy.

If you have dreamt of catching a fox in a trap, you should guard against a silly quarrel with close friends.

If you have seen yourself surprising a fox in the act of killing chickens or some other domesticated animal, you must be alert to the threat of thievery. Should you have sighted many foxes engaged in this slaughter, your guide is warning you that you have many enemies. If you happened to have killed a fox (or foxes) preying on the animals, you will succeed in all important undertaking in your life.

A dream in which you have tamed a fox and are showing it off to other people offers a sign from your guide that you have misplaced your affections and may soon suffer a disappointment in love.

GERONIMO Even if some of the actual facts of his life are a bit hazy, Geronimo's name is one of the most well-known of all American Indian chiefs. Most often portrayed as a brilliant, but cruel, Apache war chief, Geronimo was a highly regarded Medicine Priest of the Chiricahua, who spent most of his long life attempting to make an honorable peace with the white man.

Born about 1829 near the headwaters of the Gila River in New Mexico into the tribe of the Bedonkohe Apaches, his easy-going nature was reflected in his name, *Goyanthlay*, One Who Yawns. It was not until Mexican troops murdered his family in 1858 that the young man was transformed into a vengeful warrior. For whatever reason, the Mexicans nicknamed the fiery Apache, Geronimo (Jerome), and it was by that name that he became the most feared Indian in the Mexico-Arizona frontier.

In the 1860s, Geronimo joined the Chiricahuas, remarried, and joined forces with Cochise. For over a decade the two great warriors, outmanned and outgunned, managed to keep both the U.S. and the Mexican armies outfought. When Cochise surrendered in 1872, Geronimo rejected the terms of the peace treaty and led renegade raids into Mexico and Arizona until he was arrested by U.S. authorities in 1877.

Sympathetic whites knew that the tough old warrior would never stay on the flaming acres of hell and sand that constituted the San Carlos reservation, and most were amazed that Geronimo tried for four years to farm the parched land before he broke out with a handful of loyal warriors.

It was Apache scouts loyal to General George Crook who tracked the renegades down in 1881, but Geronimo kept on escaping from confinement. In 1886, Geronimo was at last convinced that if he surrendered peacefully, the U.S. army would keep its word that the warriors and their families would not be separated. As soon as the holdout Chiricahua were in captivity, the army broke its promise and sent the chief and his warriors to rot in a damp Florida prison.

In 1894, eight years later, those who had survived the prison camp in Florida were transported to Fort Sill, Oklahoma. Reduced to selling trinkets and posing for photographs at expositions and fairs, Geronimo died in Oklahoma in 1909.

If you should have received images of Geronimo or experienced spirit energy that you feel might be his, you should at once enter the silence of meditation in an effort to determine precisely why this great chief's vibrations should be manifesting to you as helper or as guide. You may be receiving a message never to give up, even in the face of overwhelming odds. You may be receiving instructions to determine what you believe to be the right course, then to stick with it regardless of whatever opposition arises to confront you.

GIFT Everyone loves to receive a gift, but the ancient admonitions urging caution toward certain of the gift-givers remain strongly in force.

If your dream scenario depicted you receiving many extravagant gifts from a single individual who professed to be a great admirer, beware in your waking reality of the motives of the allegedly generous person. If in the dream you should have reciprocated by presenting the multiple gift-giving with a present, you will probably be in for a run of bad luck.

If you receive a gift from a loved one, you may expect success in a forthcoming venture.

If your night vision portrayed you receiving a gift from a celebrity or an important person in your particular field of endeavor, you may expect to receive honors from a high source.

A dream in which you are giving gifts to relatives indicates that you have high hopes for your future.

GUN To dream of carrying a gun concealed on your person is to receive a warning from your guide that you are entering into dangerous surroundings wherein many enemies--hidden and revealed--await you.

A dream in which you have bought a firearm signals an increase in your earnings. If someone presents you with a firearm in a dream, you will soon receive a significant honor.

A night vision in which you have shot a stranger with a gun presents a warning that you may be dishonored by some sort of indiscriminate action in your waking reality. If the scenario had you shooting a known enemy, then you may be on the verge of a law suit.

If you dreamt that you were shot by a stranger, you are liable to be coming down with a serious illness. If you also fired upon and struck your assailant, a loved one may soon pass away.

HAIR The Indians wore their hair in various styles, and only recently has Hollywood taken notice that not all tribes wore their hair braided in pigtails. The Dakota wore their hair long, parted it in the middle, and wrapped and braided two long strands at the sides of the face. Some tribes, such as certain of the Iroquois and Pawnee clipped their hair short, then formed a "horn" of the scalp lock which they made rigid with animal fat. Other people, such as the Nez Perce, wore their hair shoulder-length and loose. Young Hopi women wore the "squash blossom" whorl over each ear until the plain braids of marriage replaced the more elaborate hairdo.

As with other traditional people, many Medicine Priests believed that human hair possessed magical properties. Hair had to do with a man's strength and virility, with a woman's attractiveness and power--and with at least a portion of the soul of each of them. Most scholars now concede that, generally speaking, the grisly practice of taking scalps was initiated by the white allies of the Indians as a means of tallying the correct number of enemies that the tribal warriors had slain, thereby providing them with accurate payment of their bloodmoney.

If you have dreamed of your hair thinning or falling out, you may soon be experiencing great emotional sorrow. If you perceived your hair turning rapidly gray, you will probably undergo a separation from your family.

A dream in which you groom your hair and are satisfied with the result foreshadows a new love interest in your life.

A man who dreams of wearing his hair very long wishes to be treated with dignity in his waking state.

A woman who dreams of becoming bald will soon experience financial losses.

A dream scenario that involves your hair becoming snarled and tangled is liable to anticipate an unpleasant legal action of lengthy duration.

Should you dream of growing your hair so long that it matches the length of your body, your guide is probably warning you that you are being deceived by your love partner.

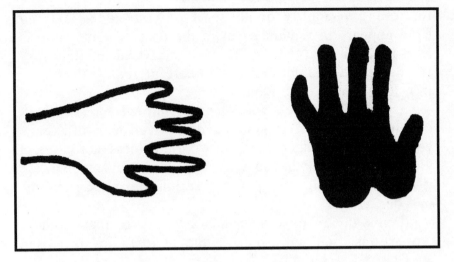

HAND   Among the tribes of North America, the human hand represented supplication to the Master of Life, the Great Mystery. Medicine Priests are almost always depicted in pictoglyphs with their hands uplifted and outstretched. The hand could also represent strength, power, and mastery.

In Christian symbology, the uplifted hand in art emphasizes the thumb (stout and strong, the Chief Person of the Godhead), the third finger (the tallest finger, Christ, the most important member for human salvation), and the second finger (the Holy Spirit, proceeding from the Father and the Son).

Throughout the tribes of the Americas, from the Mayas to the Mohicans, one quite often notices the prints of a red hand with thumbs and fingers extended on everything from horses' flanks to rifle stocks. A general kind of consensus suggests that these seals were employed to ward off evil and that originally they symbolized the flaming sun.

If you have received a dream from your guide in which your own hands were emphasized in the action of the scenario, you have been given a sign of the accord that exists between you and your love partner.

A dream in which one's hand appears to shrink is

foretelling infidelity on the part of your lover. If your hand appears to remain clean in the dream, your guide is assuring you that you will overcome these difficulties. If your hand becomes dirty, be careful that your relationship is not destroyed.

A dream in which your hand is burned foreshadows the loss of friends. If your hand received a painful cut, you will incur many debts in your business activities. If your hands are tied, you will be at a disadvantage when it comes to straightening out a serious misunderstanding in your work.

If you dream of your hands swelling to mammoth proportions, you will soon be the recipient of increased wealth.

If a stranger appears in the dream drama and kisses your hands, you will receive friendship and good fortune from new, and unexpected, friends.

Handsome Lake

The winter of 1799 was an especially bitter one in the woodlands of upper state New York. The Iroquois Confederacy of six nations--Mohawk, Oneida, Cayuga, Seneca, Onondaga, and Tuscarora -- had pledged their fortunes to the wrong side in the War of the Revolution, and now military defeat, punitive land confiscations, the spread of a general despondency, and the use of alcohol threatened to crumble the once proud warriors and their finely structured culture.

It was at that time that the Great Mystery touched Handsome Lake (*Ganiodaivo*] in a dream and gave him a message to share with his people. The spirit master commanded the Iroquois to forsake the white man's liquor and the easy divorce laws that weak tribal members had created to satisfy their own lusts. Furthermore, the spirit master forbade the sale of any more tribal lands to the white man. No one owned any part of the Earth Mother, and unscrupulous chiefs were pretending to sell pieces of her in order to finance great drunken orgies. The Great Mystery told Handsome Lake to instruct his brothers and sisters that it was now time to practice the old virtues of industry and thrift that had been abandoned with the coming of the white man. And the Iroquois must cease at once their participation in the new cults of evil witchcraft that were rising in their midst.

Handsome Lake stung his listeners with a powerful indictment of the bad ways into which they had fallen. The Great Spirit had given him a message that his followers called *Ga Wiio*, the Good Word. And that good word was a call to the Iroquois to reinstate the former values that had made their nation so great.

The Iroquois had to remember the old teachings that had made them revere the land as sacred, a gift from the Great Mystery that had been presented not only to those living then, but to the generations of unborn. The Master of Life, the Upholder of the Sky, blended energies with the Earth Mother to give them the corn, the beans, and the squash, the great Supporters of Life, the Three Sisters from the plant kingdom.

Among the Iroquois, women belonged a society known as the Sisters of the Sustainers, whose duty it was to revere the earth and to gather the rich harvest that the Master of Life provided. To celebrate the abundance with which they had been blessed, it was the custom of the Iroquois to hold such festivals as Thanks to the Maple and the Cornplanting Festival.

But now, Handsome Lake admonished them, instead of giving thanks to the Master of Life for sparing their lives in the American colonists' war against the British, the Iroquois warriors spent their time in drunken sport and slothful ways. If they would live again like men, masters of their own land, chiefs of their own destiny, they must return to the old ways.

The message of Handsome Lake spread like wildfire among his people. Hundreds of desperate Iroquois gathered before the long houses to hear the Good Wood that the prophet had brought from the Great Mystery.

Handsome Lake admonished them that they could once again be a proud people and break free of the encircling chains of the white man.

One of Handsome Lake's meetings provided his followers with a full day of spiritual experiences. The mornings were given to a recitation by Handsome Lake of all the glories that had been achieved by the Iroquois in the days when they had lived according to the laws of the Master of Life. At noon, a great feast was held, as a symbolic promise of the abundance that would soon return if the Six Nations would once again return to the paths of righteousness. During the afternoon session, the lessons of the morning talks would be discussed again and examined in greater detail. Men and women were asked to count their sins on strings of wampum, to confess them openly, and promise never to commit the transgressions again. At night, another great feast would be held to celebrate the new path on which they had placed themselves by deciding to follow the Good Word. The ancient drums would beat, and the old tribal dances would occupy the joyful Iroquois until the dawn.

Handsome Lake's inspired dream had come upon him in the winter of 1799 and until his death in 1815, the preacher spread the Good Word among thousands of Iroquois in the Six Nations confederacy. Those who refused to heed his words of reformation fell victim to the unquenchable hunger of the white man for more land and the inevitable demand that the Indian move on to other camp grounds. As often as not, the Iroquois who had not heard the Good Word would be swindled out of their birthright for a few gallons of firewater or a handful of shiny trinkets.

Cynics might argue that Fate was not a great deal kinder to the followers of the Good Word, but they were able to confront their destiny with a dignity that they had learned from the passionate teachings of Handsome Lake, the messenger of the Master of Life.

If you have become aware of thoughts, images, and inspirations from a source that you believe to be the spirit energy of Handsome Lake, it would behoove you to undergo a process of serious self-evaluation and self-discipline before you enter the silence of deep meditation in order to determine the exact reason why such a powerful vibration has made contact with you. You should carefully analyze the messages that you have received for any Medicine symbols that may add clarification to the communications which you have received. Quite likely, you are being alerted to be of meaningful service to the Earth Mother and all of her children.

HAWK The Iowa Indians so revered a particular species of hawk that they only killed it on rare occasions in order to obtain certain portions of its body to place with their most sacred medicines. The Iowas believed that the hawk had a supernatural faculty that enabled it to remain indefinitely on the wing and to fly directly to the land of spirits. A chant expressed the sentiments thusly:

> The hawks turned their heads nimbly 'round
> They turn to look back on their flight.
> The spirits have whispered them words;
> They fly with their messages swift,
> They look as they fearfully go,
> They look to the furthermost end of the world,
> Their eyes glancing light, and their beaks boding harm.

In Egypt, hawks were kept in the temple of the Sun-god where the deity himself was represented as a man with a hawk's head encircled by the disk of the sun. The Greeks considered the hawk sacred to the Great Light, and the Romans associated the bird with Jupiter, Lord of the Gods, and referred to the hawk as the Great Light of the Father.

If your quest has revealed the hawk to be your

Tlingit representation
of the Thunderbird.

totem animal, then its appearance in any of your dreams will signal you to take note of a series of important symbols that will be certain to follow. These symbols will be special messages issuing from your guide that are especially designed to assist you in making difficult decisions. After you have taken note of them, you should ponder each of them by taking them into the silence of contemplation.

A dream of a hawk soaring above you is a symbol that your fortunes will change for the better.

Should you have viewed a flock of hawks in your dream, you must be very careful concerning your business speculations.

If you shoot a hawk, you will be able to conquer seemingly insurmountable obstacles.

If you dream of holding a hawk in your hands, you will soon experience the pleasure of a great accomplishment. If you are only observing another person holding a hawk, you must be alert to enemies who are envious of you.

HIAWATHA Although the famous poem by Longfellow creates characters and situations that sprang full-blown from the artistic imagination, Hiawatha was an actual chieftain of the Turtle clan of the Mohawk. Longfellow took a number of the accomplishments of this remarkable chief and wove them into the national myths of the tribes of the Iroquois Confederacy. Later, because of the respect given to the mythic hero, Hiawatha became the hereditary name and title of Turtle clan chiefs.

Hiawatha, the Wise Man, was highly regarded as a Medicine Priest of awesome abilities. As early as 1634, an Onondaga chief told a London journalist that the mysterious Hiawatha had a canoe which would move without paddles and was obedient to his every thought. Attaining culture bearer status, it was said that it was from Hiawatha that the people learned to raise corn and beans and to attain mastery over the great monsters which haunted the fishing grounds and the darkest parts of the forest. Hiawatha pronounced wise teachings and laws directly from the Great Mystery, and before he had chosen to become human, Hiawatha had been second only to the Great Mystery in power.

The Turtle clan is the peace clan; and the first known historical Hiawatha, who lived around 1570, was devoted to the task of instituting a policy of tribal union that could evolve into a permanent government. The original Hiawatha is considered to be one of the founders of the Iroquois Confederacy, an instrument of democracy so finely devised that a great many of its principles were incorporated into the new government that was being formulated by the Founding Fathers of the United States.

A translation of the chant that the early historian Horatio Hale termed the "National Hymn of the Iroquois" is hereby quoted from *The Book of Iroquois Rites* (circa mid-1800s):

> I come again to greet and thank the League:
> I come again to greet and thank the kindred;
> I come again to greet and thank the warriors;
> I come again to greet and thank the women.
> My forefathers--what they established!
> My forefathers--hearken to them!

If you should have received thoughts, images, inspirations that you believe are somehow linked to the spirit energy of the great Hiawatha, you should prepare yourself to go deep into the silence to determine the reasons why you have been chosen for such a psychic alignment. You may have been contacted in order to alert your higher consciousness to the mission that you chose to come to the planet to fulfill. If the energy transmissions are clearly identified in your belief construct to be emanating from Hiawatha, prepare yourself for meaningful service to the Earth Mother and all of her children.

HORN When American Indians decorated their head-dresses, war bonnets, and Medicine hats with horns, especially those of the buffalo, they joined a universal tradition that employs horns as a symbol of masculine power and virility. The concept of the Horned God is as basic and primeval as the Stone Age. A cave painting made over 15,000 years ago in southern France depicts an ancient shaman wearing a horned headdress, becoming one with the spirit of the four-leggeds.

Pictoglyph of a good spirit being. The horned headress denotes that the entity has great power, further illustrated by its capture of an evil serpent.

A study of the old religions will easily demonstrate that the most distinguishing characteristic feature of a deity used to be a pair of horns growing from the head. If an entity were divine, then it must wear horns. Even the mighty Hebrew prophet, Moses, as sculpted by the great Michelangelo, is given a pair of small horns to signify his transformative experience while obtaining the Ten Commandments from Yahweh atop Mount Sinai.

If you should dream of wearing a headdress with two large horns, you will soon--if you have not already--make a strong commitment to follow a spiritual path that incorporates the principles of Medicine Power.

If the dream scenario has pictured you with horns growing directly from your head, you will proceed on your spiritual path with dignity, having dominion over the negative energies that will seek to sway you from serving the light. If you bear only one horn, you must work very hard to identify and to correct a spiritual weakness that will prevent your attaining full illumination.

If you should have perceived another person with horns growing from his or her forehead, you must be alert to someone close to you who is in danger of developing a fatal illness.

Should you experience a dream in which you find yourself confronted by satyr-like beings with large horns on their heads, your guide has offered you a symbol to prepare you for personal sorrow. If the satyrs were fitted with small horns, you may expect joy and happiness.

If the dream drama has a scene in which you are presented with a headdress that bears unusually large buffalo horns, you should be wary of an argument with a close friend that could get out of hand. If the buffalo horns got progressively smaller throughout the dream, you and your friend will reconcile your differences before hard feelings can occur.

HORSE The horse was introduced to the American Indians by the Spanish explorers in the early 1500s. Although the large, "bizarre animal" had been foreseen in the visions of such prophets as Viracocha and the greatest of the Medicine Priests, few of the people were prepared for the encounter with the awesome creature. Coronado brought the first horses to the Plains Indians in 1541. The Hopi had their introduction to the incredible four-leggeds when Antonio de Espejo visited their villages. The eastern tribes and the Iroquois Confederacy did not have their visions of the strange animal fulfilled until the early 1600s.

Typical of the tribes along the routes of the early explorers, the Blackfeet had no words to describe the great steeds on which the armored strangers sat astride. They decided the mysterious four-legged beast looked more like an elk than anything else they had seen in their world, so they named the horse, the Medicine Elk.

There should be little surprise that the horse would soon become both a sacred and a prized possession for the Indian and would begin to figure largely in his myths and legends. After all, the horse had long been a revered animal in Europe and in the Middle East. In old France, a flower-laden horse served as the symbol for the Divine Mind and Reason in various ceremonies. The traditional nursery rhyme that tells of a White Lady who rides a white horse and whose bells make music wherever she goes is quite likely referring to our Lady of Wisdom. The great philosopher Plato stated that the horse at its best signified reason coursing through the natural flow of things, and at its worst represented fantasy.

In ancient Babylon, the horse was identified with the god Zu. The Greek word for horse is *ikkos*, the "great light." The Hebrew word for horse means also "to explain," thus again equating the horse with the intellect. The Latin, *equus*, resolves into the light of the great mind or soul. The Greeks placed their god of wisdom in a chariot drawn by four fiery horses.

For many tribes, a vision of a great white horse became the symbol of Death coming to accompany the spirit to the land of the grandparents. To associate a white horse with such ethereal and holy tasks seems to have assumed the status of a universal image wherever the horse is known. The Mohammedans have their Al Borak, a milk-white steed whose single stride can place him equal to the farthest range of human vision. Slavic legends tell of Prince Slugobyl, who enlists the aid of the Invisible Knight and his horse Magu (magus, wizard), a magic white horse with a golden mane.

The Hindus Vishnu's final manifestation will occur when he reappears on a white horse with a drawn sword to restore the order of righteousness. The Book of Revelation says that Christ shall return riding upon a white horse and leading armies of righteousness seated upon white horses.

If your quest has revealed the horse as your totem animal, then its appearance in a dream will signal the advent of a series of symbols that will have special meaning to you. These symbols will be transmitted to you by your guide and a careful examination of the personal meaning of the symbols will aid you in making important decisions in dealing with problems that may beset your life path.

To dream of riding a horse and being thrown is to be given a sign that you should use more caution in your personal and business ventures.

If you dream of someone approaching you on horseback, you may expect good news soon.

If the dream scenario has employed the symbol of your observing a horse being shod, you will be the recipient of financial gains.

To view a horse running away from you is to be shown a sign of approaching disappointment and misfortune. If someone catches that horse and hitches it to a carriage, the misfortune will be overcome and happiness will be restored.

A dream drama in which you see yourself on the

back of a bucking, untamed horse that you ride into domesticity provides you with a message that you must work hard in order to achieve a particular goal.

If you perceived a friend turning his or her back to you and riding away from you, be alert to the situation that a friend (not necessarily the one shown in the dream) has romantic designs on your spouse.

If your dream scenario had your riding a limping horse into the middle of a stream, you should prepare for opposition to your goals from an unexpected quarter.

To dream of a herd of wild horses is to be given a good sign that your business transactions or the achievement of personal goals will progressively become more positive.

Reverse pictoglyph of the celebrated White Horse near Shrivenham in Berkshire, England.

ILLNESS If you have dreamed of suffering from an illness, your guide may be preparing you for a misfortune in your affairs of the heart.

If you have dreamt of visiting strangers who are suffering from an illness, you have received a sign that you will attain your goals.

A dream in which your children come down with an illness offers you a symbol of consolation and happiness. Should the dream have featured close relatives, it signals approaching unhappiness. If the dream drama focuses on your enemies and they are viewed as ill, you must guard against a temptation that could overcome you.

If your night vision concerns itself with the illness of your sweetheart, you will be liable to have to forego some pleasure to which you have been looked forward.

Should you have viewed a large number of people languishing in a hospital with a wide variety of illnesses, you will soon receive joy in your life and prosperity in your business transactions.

JOSEPH Chief Joseph is the remarkable warrior who, in 1877, led 600 of his tribe in a 1,600-mile running duel with the U.S. army in a valiant effort to reach the Canadian border and freedom for his people, the Nez Perce. Deceived into signing away their rights to their sacred Wallowa Valley in Oregon, the Nez Perce were to be relocated in Idaho. A man of peace, Joseph kept his angry warriors in check and prepared the tribe for the journey to a site that none of the Nez Perce found inviting.

Then, just before the march was to begin, a large number of Nez Perce horses were stolen, and the angry young war chiefs decided that injury had been added to insult. Eighteen white settlers were killed in retaliation for the stolen horses, and travel plans to Idaho were immediately revised. Chief Joseph agreed with his warriors' decision to rebel against the soldiers, and he set out to lead his people to safety in Canada.

After evading the heavily-armed pursuing U.S. Army for 1,600 miles and checkmating the superior force in thirteen battles, Chief Joseph was finally forced to surrender when his tribe was only thirty miles from the Canadian border. The noble chief's surrender speech as been often quoted and it reads in part as follows:

> "I am tired of fighting...It is cold and we have no blankets. The little children are freezing to death...I want to have time to look for my children and see how many of them I can find. Maybe I shall find them among the dead. Hear me, my chiefs. I am tired; my heart is sick and sad. From where the sun now stands, I will fight no more forever."

The survivors of the incredible running battle were sent to Kansas. Chief Joseph died on September 21, 1904, at Nespelem on the Colville Reservation in Washington.

If you believe that you may have received thoughts, images, or inspirations from the spirit energy of the great Chief Joseph, you should prepare yourself to go deep into the silence to determine the reasons why you have been contacted by such a powerful vibration. You may have been touched by this entity in order to alert your higher consciousness to the mission that you chose to come to the planet to fulfil. Examine any messages received for more precise clues for the interaction which may be occurring between you and Chief Joseph.

JOURNEY A dream in which you set out on a long, pleasant journey provides you with a symbol of important success about to be achieved after a period of hard work. If you saw yourself on horseback, you will be certain to surmount all obstacles strewn in your path. If you perceived yourself as having to walk all the way, be prepared for very hard work ahead on the path to your goal.

If the journey was to be accomplished by traveling in an airplane, be braced for family quarrels to beset you on the trek toward some important goal on the physical plane. If you set out by a car, you should receive abundantly. If the journey was to be achieved aboard a ship, you will enjoy harmony among you and your friends while you experience hard work on the path to your success.

LAKE Dreams of lakes, ponds, and other bodies of water very often yield remarkable insights into one's psyche and the depths and potentials of one's creative self.

If you have dreamed of wading in a muddy lake, your thoughts are unclear and you are likely to experience confusion and unhappiness in your acts of creative expression.

If the lake was seen as clear, however, you may expect to achieve success rather easily.

If you envisioned yourself sailing on the lake, be on guard against things appearing too easy and sudden conflicts that may break out on the domestic scene.

If your boat had no sail and you were forced to row across the lake, you have received a symbol of success to be achieved.

If you stopped rowing and began to fish in the lake, you will be recognized with an advancement in your professional life.

A dream in which rain began to fall on you while you were moving across the lake has provided you with a calming symbol that you will overcome all of your worries if you exercise patience.

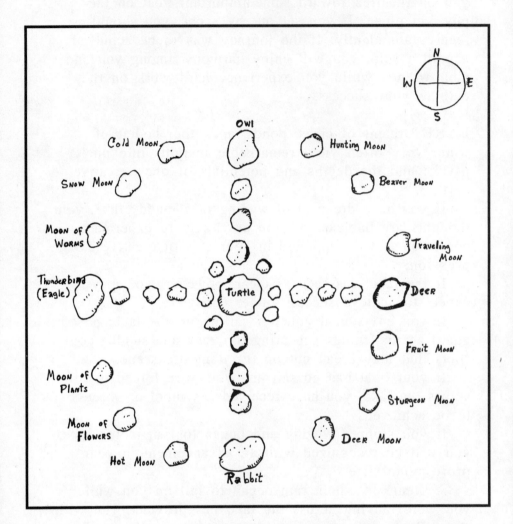

Authors Medicine Hawk and Grey Cat [*American Indian Ceremonies*s, Inner Light] state that the Medicine Wheel is a spiritual sending and receiving device, "a transcendental teaching and learning instrument" which can become the universe to the seeker. There is no one set, dogmatic layout to the Medicine Wheel. The one illustrated here is a blend of a number of tribal cosmologies.

Medicine Wheel

Often as you stand in that haunted, sacred place, you swear that you can hear the whisper of faraway drums. Sometimes, there is also a softly heard chant that seems to ride the gray veil of fog that covers the east summit of Big Horn Mountain in the morning and settle just above the mysterious circle of stone that should not be there.

Efforts to explain the enigma of the Medicine Wheel of the Big Horn Mountains continues to challenge the intellectually adventurous. Anthropologists have declared that their very existence in North America seems contrary to every known fact that we have learned about our early inhabitants. Archaeologists have not even been able to identify a suitable culture to which they might attribute the giant enigma.

The Medicine Wheel forms an almost perfect circle 70 feet in diameter and 245 feet in circumference. Its "hub" is 12 feet in diameter with a seven—foot opening in its middle. Twenty-eight stone "spokes" reach out from the axis to the outer rim of the wheel. Six large monuments are located around the rim, and other monuments have been built on high points of land at some distance from the wheel. The whole mammoth creation is located high on the tops of the windswept Big Horn Mountains of Wyoming. No one knows who built the wheel, not even the Indians.

"It is of prehistoric origin," said a well-educated historian of the Shoshone. "Our people say that it was there long before our fathers came to the land. The Crows believed that the wheel was the work of the Great Mystery who dropped it down from the sky."

The Medicine Wheel is not unlike the strange religious megalithic rims built by forgotten cults of primitive Europe, and it is curiously similar to great ceremonial calendar wheels constructed in Mexico by the Aztecs. Even more startling, according to some experts, is the suggestion that some of the engineering principles it exhibits might only have been learned in ancient Egypt.

Certain authorities have fixed the date of the wheel's construction all the way from 15,000 to 1,000 B.C. The Aztecs, the Mayans, even the Druids of Great Britain, the alleged builders of Stonehenge, have been named as possible constructors of the strange wheel.

In an 1895 issue of *Field and Stream* magazine, the author speculated that the wheel had been constructed by a vanished race akin to the Aztecs, and he noted the similarity between the Big Horn Wheel and the calendar stone circles believed to be the work of that ancient Mexican culture.

One thing is certain--the Indians did not build it. The Big Horn mountains held special significance for the Crow, the Sioux, the Arapaho, the Shoshone, and the Cheyenne—-any of whom *might* have erected the Medicine Wheel--but none of these tribes of the mountains and the plains ever constructed anything of stone——not houses, not forts, not temples, not even tombstones.

The Big Horn Wheel is older than the memory of those tribes, and although some came to know of the wheel later and adopted its use for their own ceremonies, they knew clearly that their own ancestors had not built the strange shrine.

Who did build it? Perhaps we'll never know. If it had been discovered in the Alps, the mystery would not have seemed so undecipherable. Such an artifact would more easily fit with what we know about the primitive inhabitants of Europe. But a huge stone wheel in the Big Horn Mountains is as alien a thing as a stretch of desert at the North Pole.

Bits of wood found in one of the six smaller cairns situated unevenly about the rim indicates that the wheel has been there since at least 1760. The monument has been known to the whitemen since the 1870s, but conjecture about its true purpose has only inspired legends and tall tales.

Certain of those legends tell that the mysterious wheel was built "in the time before iron" by a shadowy race of people that lowland tribes had never seen and who left behind them not one other memento of their reign in the Big Horns.

Real scientific investigation of the wheel did not begin until 1902 when a Field Columbian Museum party led by S.C. Simms took up the challenge. Although Simms made many inquiries about the Medicine Wheel of the old men of the Crow tribe, he found "not one" who had ever visited it. A few of the senior members of the tribe had heard of the wheel from their fathers, but they could tell Simms nothing whatever, "except it was made by people who had no iron."

In the June 7, 1974 issue of *Science*, astronomer John A. Eddy of the High Altitude Observatory in Boulder, Colorado, said that two summers' research had convinced him that the Big Horn Monument may well have been an ancient astronomical observatory that served its creators at least as well as Stonehenge served its primitive astronomers. The high altitude (9,640 feet) and the clear horizons of the monument make easily visible the marking of sunrise and sunset at the summer solstice. The accurate knowledge of the first day of summer would have been a most important bit of intelligence for a nomadic people whose very lives depended upon an astute awareness of seasonal changes.

It does seem quite certain that the lost tribe of craftsmen who built the Medicine Wheel may have been sun worshippers and chose the towering mountain area to be closer to that deity and to shroud their ritual in the safe accessibility of the peak.

Incorporated in the construction of the rim is what appears to be a deliberately engineered break in the structure oriented toward capturing the first rays of the morning sun. That aspect of the riddle may well mean that the ancient builders of the shrine had developed astronomical calculations at a time when Europe was still slumbering in the trance of prehistory.

The famous Crow battle chief Red Plume, who ruled his tribe when Lewis and Clark were mapping the

North American continent, is said to have gone to the Medicine Wheel to be instructed by the Great Spirit in the martial arts and he is supposed to have taken his name from the red-plumed eagles that soar above the lonely mesa.

Tribes who came long after the original wheel makers have recognized the site as one where the Great Spirit may be present and may choose to communicate with the devout.

Today, a Medicine Wheel–wherever it is constructed–is considered a place for spiritual communion.

MONTEZUMA Throughout Mexico and North America--and especially among the tribes of the Southwest--Montezuma, the great emperor of the Aztecs, has achieved culture-bearer status nearly the equal of the legendary Quetzalcoatl. People as far north as the Blackfeet are certain that Montezuma would have ruled all of the Americas if it had not been for the treachery of the Spanish invaders.

The legends state, however, that because he was such a master sorcerer, Montezuma achieved the ability to return freely in his spirit body after his death and to work even greater miracles than when he was alive.

Montezuma's spirit energy is usually associated with white magic, and reverence for the Aztec leader has very often become a form of religious expression for the members of many tribes. In earlier times, the harder the Roman Catholic missionaries attempted to stamp out the virtual worship of Montezuma, the greater his stature as a protector of the native religion was assured. The more fiercely the priests tried to identify Montezuma as a devil, the more benevolent he seemed to a people oppressed by the "black robes" and their god of wrath.

The historical Montezuma ruled the Aztec Empire from 1503 until his death in 1520. In folk myth, he was born among the Rio Grande Indians and became recognized as a mighty ruler and priest in the Pueblo of Pecos. A mystic who possessed unparalleled supernatural powers, he took a Zuni girl as his bride and queen, then mounted a giant eagle to fly south in order to build Tenochtitlan (Mexico City) the capital of his empire. The Pueblo and other southwestern tribes may first have heard of Montezuma through the Spanish soldiers who could have boasted of their conquest of the Aztec emperor as a kind of object lesson, graphically illustrating what might be expected by those Indians who opposed their quest for gold. What stuck in the minds of the tribes of the Southwest, however, was not the lesson of how cruelly the Spaniards had dealt with the Aztecs, but the mystique of Montezuma, the wonder worker of magic. Scholars have observed that the Aztec leader became incorporated into the folklore and tradition of the Pueblo Indians in an astonishingly brief period of time. From New Mexico, tales of the magical feats of Montezuma spread to other tribes. It was not long before people were healing in Montezuma's name, blessing the hunt in his name, and growing corn in his name.

If you believe that you may have received thoughts, images, inspirations, and visions from the spirit entity known as Montezuma, you should undergo a brief fast, then prepare to enter the silence in order to determine why you may have been selected to enter a spiritual alignment with the vibrations of the great mystic emperor of the Aztecs. You may have been contacted in order to alert your higher consciousness to the true reasons why you chose to incarnate on the Earth Mother. Carefully analyze the messages that you believe to be emanating from this powerful spirit energy.

MOON The name of the moon in one Indian dialect can mean either I *sleep* or *I die*, an association of concepts that seems to epitomize the profound role of the moon in the cosmology of the red man. The moon was the ruling spirit that turned night into day and shepherded souls of the deceased into another dimension of reality.

The feminine spirit of the
Moon pictured above land and
water.

The native people of North and South America lifted their eyes to behold the wonder of the evening sky and saw everywhere the handiwork of the Great Mystery.

It soon became apparent that Sister Moon turned her face to them in a cycle that could be reckoned, month after month, year after year. Simple calculations began to form in the minds of those who watched the stars, and they saw that the seasons changed their sparkling night-time sky raiment as well as their day-time earth coverings.

To the Sioux, the moon was an old friend who helped them number the passage of seasons and events important to their lives. Beginning a cycle that followed the spring equinox's first full moon, the Sioux developed a calendar of months which they named the Moon of Worms, the Moon of Plants, the Moon of Flowers, the Warm Moon, the Moon of the Deer, the Moon of the Sturgeon, the Moon of Corn, the Moon of Journeys, the Beaver's Moon, the Hunting Moon, the Cold Moon, and the Moon of Snow. For the Sioux, the concept of time had been born.

Some tribes, with less poetry and less curiosity than the Sioux, fashioned primitive calendars in which only the months thought favorable were designated, from the first warmth of spring to the rich harvests of autumn. The cruel winter months were omitted and left dead and unnamed.

Throughout the ancient traditions of Europe, the moon was regarded as feminine, and the moon goddess, with her control over many cycles of creation, including women's menstrual cycles, was considered the creator of time. In the early days of the white settlement of North America, the missionaries and traders found that the Indians also utilized the various changes of the moon as a method of measuring time, but there were variables as to the names of the "months." The elders of certain tribes disputed among themselves how many moons there were in each year. Drawing largely upon the Chippewa tradition, one scholar delineated the moons in the following list:

> March, the green moon; April, the moon of plants; May, the moon of flowers; June, the hot moon; July, the moon of the deer; August, the sturgeon moon; September, the fruit moon; October, the traveling moon; November, the beaver moon; December, the hunting moon; January, the cold moon; February, the snowy moon. (Some tribes, after counting twelve moons for the year, add a thirteenth, which they call "the lost moon.")

Other traditions, such as the Egyptian, have given the moon a prominent role in the act of creation, in some instances naming her "Mother of the Universe." The Babylonians gave the moon dominance over the sun, and numerous Oriental cultures worshipped the moon over the sun, for the goddess of the moon gave her light at night, when humankind really needed it, while the sun chose to shine only by day.

The moon at crescent, "with a white band around her throat."

A Jesuit missionary recorded the words of one Medicine Priest who saw the moon as an old woman who never died. "She keeps watch over all our actions, and she wears a white band around her throat (referring to the white line of the crescent)." This shaman believed the moon to have six children: the eldest was day; the next younger, the sun; the youngest, night. The daughters of the moon were the stars that corresponded to the polar star, Venus, and the morning star.

Certain tribes believed that the moon gathered up the souls of the human female dead. Women, reasoned the shaman, are curious by nature, and the habits of the moon spirit were compatible with their own.

A number of tribes portray the moon giving birth to the four winds and to elder spirits who inhabited the earth before the advent of humankind. The moon, for many Medicine Priests, remained the determiner of one's longevity and the guardian over the transmigration of the human soul.

If your dream drama has portrayed your viewing a full moon, you will be assured of a great enjoyment of your future. The brighter the illumination from the full moon, the happier will be the coming days. If there were a few clouds that moved across the face of the full moon, you should be prepared to deal with the occasional interruption in your tranquility. If the sky was free of clouds in your dream of the full moon, your successes will be almost completely uncluttered.

A woman who dreams of leaning over the bank of pool of water and sees her reflection in its surface will soon fall in love with the man of her dreams.

A man who dreams of being illuminated by moon glow will find his soul mate.

Should the dream scenario depict the moon falling from the sky, you must be prepared for a great loss of money.

A blood-red moon that appears in your dream presents a warning of approaching strife.

If the night vision portrays you observing a moon that suddenly becomes dark, be advised of the illness of a mother, a sister, a daughter, or your wife.

If you dream of making a voyage to the moon, you should re-examine your goals to determine if you might not have set your temporary achievement level a bit too high.

Time was measured by the various North American tribes with greater and lesser degrees of accuracy. From their continued observation of the moon and their noting that a cycle of months might be calculated, the majority of Indian tribes conceived the periods of days that passed between the changing of the moon and formulated the concept of a twelve-month cycle in which some 360 days passed and four distinct seasons altered the structure of their world.

But it was the amazing Mayan astronomers of Central America that developed a calendar that remains to this day a testimony to an incredible mathematical skill--a skill which contributed to our own modern concepts of measuring time.

Before the time of Christ, the Mayas had fashioned a towering culture that stretched across those large portions of Central America that now comprise all of Guatemala and British Honduras, as well as parts of El Salvador, Honduras, and Mexico. The great Mayas carved massive cities, sometimes covering thousands of acres, out of the teeming jungles; and they left behind huge burial pyramids that strangely mirror the great pyramids of Egypt. Theoretical minds of awesome genius were at work among the Maya during the period between 350 B.C. to about 900 A.D.--a time that historians agree forged the apex of the highly complex Mayan culture. The intellectuals among the Mayas employed logic, as well as abstract philosophical concepts; and they developed a hieroglyphic system for recording their thoughts. In addition, they structured a highly accurate arithmetic that included the use of the zero.

It was in astronomy that the Mayas achieved their greatest intellectual accomplishment when they developed a calendar so precise that their mathematicians were capable of handling calculations based on innumerable thousands and of achieving a measuring stick of time on which a million years could be calculated.

What astonishes modern astronomers most is the demonstrable fact that the early Mayan astronomers had devised a calendrical concept that contemporary mathematicians have termed "the long count," a device that permitted the Maya to record the passage of days with an unerring accuracy that rivals modern science's best efforts. The so-called long count was created to reconcile the two separate calendars which the Maya had fashioned--one to designate the civil year of 365 days; the second to make the magic cycle of Tzolkin, a year of 260 holy days.

By use of the long count, the Mayan astronomers were able to reckon back to the date 3114 B.C.--although historians cannot agree whether or not the Mayan calendar had been developed at that time. Controversy also rages over the question of why the Maya strove to create a calendar that would be able to record days so deep in antiquity. What would have been the purpose of the Mayan astronomers to seek to examine a world before their own?

While some scholars argue over the "why" of the Mayan calendar, others are simply stunned by the clear reality that they most certainly did possess it. And that startling fact being the case, there is a strong likelihood that if the Mayas possessed a science of astronomy capable of dating a calendar back three thousand years before Christ, then it would seem highly likely that the Mayas were even further advanced than the great Egyptian theoreticians, who are generally credited with the development of calendrical science.

At the same time, historians and anthropologists also ponder the mystery of why the Mayan calendar reaches out into years that modern man has not yet contemplated. Why did the ancient people of the Maya wish to count years by the millions and to project their thoughts so far into the future?

Yet another Mayan mystery that challenges modern science are the great stone "steles" that the Mayas left behind in the ruins of their cities. The steles, giant stone slabs erected on elevated platforms, are believed now to mark certain special time intervals that the Mayas held as particularly significant. Most scholars today believe that the steles were not raised to honor great deeds or cultural heroes, but to commemorate cosmic events witnessed in the heavens.

And again, the Mayan steles form a strange link to Egypt, where the oldest previously known examples of such monuments were raised. The remarkable discovery of both steles and pyramids in the remote jungles of Central America has led a number of serious scholars to speculate that some kind of cultural transmission must have occurred between the ancient Mayan and Egyptian people.

The brilliant scientific minds that formulated the incredible Mayan calendar and so many other remarkable concepts vanished suddenly into the mists of the Central American jungle sometime shortly after 900 A.D. Their abrupt disappearance after having made so many remarkable contributions to the intellectual evolution of the human species has prompted numerous fascinating, if far-out, theories.

Some bold thinkers have even suggested that since Quetzacoatl, the Mayas' great culture-bearer, is said to have descended from the sky in a great silver egg, he might well have been a space being, an ancient astronaut. Perhaps the marvelous Mayan civilization was an experimental colony from an other world. How else would one explain, these theorists argue, a remote Indian tribe in the center of a jungle suddenly knowing how to count the years by millions, to work complex mathematical problems involving the positional notation of numbers, and to understand the concept of completion, or zero?

In allegory, mountains represent many of the same things to the American Indian as they did to the European—a Higher Source, meditation, communion with the divine.

MOUNTAIN Great, lofty mountains were considered sacred to the tribes of the American Indian. Some legends spoke of humankind originally coming up from within the bowels of a mountain to life on the Earth Mother. Other traditions suggested powerful spirits who chose to dwell on the snowy peaks. In general, it might be said that the same awe of towering mountains that was felt by the Hebrews regarding "the mountain of Jehovah" was experienced by the tribes of America.

As the psalmist sang, "O Jehovah, who shall abide in thy tabernacle? Who shall dwell in the mountains of thy holiness?", so chanted a shaman who dwelt in the Sierra Nevada:

"I sing among the mountain flowers.
I sing among the flowering mountain bushes.
I sing in the mountains like a bird.
I sing among the rocks like a bird.
In the morning I cry in the mountains.
In the morning I walk the path.
I cry out to the spirit of the morning star."

Grandmother Twylah, Repositor of Wisdom for the Seneca, has remarked that to dream of two lofty mountain peaks is to envision your ideals on two levels of awareness--with one level shouting loudly to the sleeping face of the other to awaken.

If you have dreamt of viewing a massive, snow-covered mountain from a distance, you have been given a sign that you will soon receive a great favor.

If you have dreamed of beginning a climb to the top of a towering mountain peak, your guide has presented you with a symbol of struggle in the achievement of a goal deemed very important by you. Should you turn back half-way up, you will gain a small amount of success. If you reach the very top, you will achieve full, unfettered success in an important endeavor.

A dream in which a mountain climber stops to wave at you offers you a warning that you are about to receive a visit from a disagreeable person.

A dream scenario which depicts a fire burning on a

mountain top is foreshadowing a coming catastrophe in your life.

If you should have dreamed of a great mountain slide or avalanche, you have been shown a sign that previews the death of a prominent person.

MOUSE Grandmother Twylah of the Seneca teaches that a mouse is a symbol that one should review things that are close at hand. A dream of a mouse is a sign that you should re-examine items that you might have stored away with the notion that you might make better use of them.

Grandmother goes on to say that people who somehow identify with a mouse in a dream may be receiving guidance that while they are not be opposed in principle to sharing, they may not always be as sensitive as they should be to the needs of others. The symbol of the mouse signifies that they have a potential to expand their awareness.

OWL To the Winnebago, the owl ruled the north, the land of the unknown, of cold, dark forests, of death.

Some tribes believed that if they heard an owl calling their name, they were soon to die.

Universally, the owl is a symbol of wisdom. At the same time, the owl is always associated with witchcraft. "Wicca," the northern European title for those who practice witchcraft, means the "wise ones," and the witches of this tradition emphasize the owl as one of their principal totems.

The old Roman word for an owl is *strix*, the same as their word for a witch. The traditional celebration of Halloween would hardly be the same without the staring owls overseeing the black cats, the ghosts, and the witches.

If your visions and guidance have revealed the owl as your personal totem, then its appearance in any of your dreams will signal you to take careful notice of a series of important symbols that will be certain to follow.

These symbols will hold special messages from your guide that are especially designed to assist you in making important decisions along the pathway of your spiritual evolution.

A dream of an owl will most often signal the advent of personal unhappiness. If your dream scenario proceeds to the point where you capture the owl, you will be likely to achieve happiness. Should you kill the owl in your dream, your guide has shown you that you will persevere until you have attained great happiness and success.

If you have dreamed of seeing yourself in an eerie setting in which you can hear the faraway hoot of an owl, you have been warned of a deceitful person in your life. If that faraway hooting should draw nearer and become the shrill screeching of an owl, you are being alerted to the death of someone close to you.

Palenque

When the royal sarcophagus in the depths of the sacred Temple of Laws at ancient Palenque, Chiapas, Mexico, was opened, the scholars who set aside the massive stone slab were startled to find therein the mysteriously garbed remains of a man that science was certain should not have been there--a citizen who seemed more representative of an Egyptian, rather than a Mayan, civilization. Together with the seemingly misplaced skeletal remains were artifacts from a culture that simply did not belong there in Chiapas.

Beautifully carved jade religious accoutrements rested in the skeletal hands of the tomb's occupant. A mosaic death mask had been placed over the royal face before the huge stone lid of the sarcophagus had been sealed. A small jade religious symbol had also been inserted in the corpse's mouth by priests of a long-forgotten faith. Each of these practices seemed to reflect rites for the dead employed only by the ancient Egyptians.

The intricately fashioned death mask, made of jade, obsidian, and small bits of shell, was closely akin to the pressed paper masks that veiled the faces of rulers entombed at timeless Ur and at later Mesopotamian and Chaldean burial sites. The stones placed in the mouth of the Palenque ruler mirrored the Egyptian belief that the Ka, or the spirit of the soul, takes its final leave of the body through that orifice.

Pictoglyph of the spirit Tarenyawago, Holder of the Universe. Upon his head, the spirit bears the sacred circle of life surmounted by a symbol of the four winds.

What disconcerted the scientists the most as they stared into the sarcophagus at Palenque was the size of the ancient leader's skeleton. Measuring more than five feet, eight inches, the scholars argued that the remains were not those of a long-dead Mayan ruler, for the inhabitants of old Mexico had been much shorter. In addition, the arm measurements of the mysterious, forgotten king were found to be very long, indicative of a prehistoric or a much earlier form of man. To make matters even more complicated, the longer shape of the monarch's skull indicated that the tribe that had buried its leader in this sarcophagus practiced skull deformation upon its youth at the time of birth. As far as it is known, Mayans never used this form of ritualistic bone shaping

The king who lay in splendor at Palenque had ruled over a civilization lost to history--a civilization that had attained fantastic engineering skill at a time when it seems impossible for such architectural expertise to have existed on the continent.

The tomb in which the sarcophagus lay had been constructed of massive stones, expertly hewn and cemented together with a mortar so strong that scientists found it easier to crack the stones than the bonding agent that held them together. The sarcophagus and the huge stone slab on which it rested was estimated as weighing somewhere near twenty tons. In some unknown manner, the workmen of Palenque had managed to hoist that poundage when they placed four square stones, carved to represent faces, underneath the slab and the tomb to hold its weight for centuries.

Historically, the building of pyramids in the Americas is uniquely Mayan, part of the tradition of that amazing people who bloomed and built on the Yucatan Peninsula in a time lost to history, then inexplicably vanished somewhere near 800 A.D.

The unknown pyramid builders of Palenque flourished at an earlier age than the great Mayan societies that were to follow. These unnamed Old Ones knew secrets yet undreamed in the dawning minds of humans in the continents of Europe and Asia, and it seems certain that this elder race bore the teachers who instructed the Mayans to emulate their magnificent kingdoms in the jungles of Mexico.

Sherry Hansen Steiger meditates
on the Hub of the Universe in
Cuzco, Peru, the ancient Inca capital.

PERU Ancient Peruvian legends relate the account of Manco Capac and Mama Ogllo, two divine beings from the stars, who descended near Lake Titicaca. The star beings had been given orders to traverse the planet Earth until they found a place to sink a golden wedge that would become a culture center. The sacred wedge from the stars disappeared at Cuzco, which then became the "navel" or the "hub" of the universe. Cuzco, which means essentially, the "Mighty Light," was the capital of the great empires of the Incas.

Peru contains mysteries and miracles to boggle any mind--from its mammoth cities high in the Andes to the strange, gigantic markings on its plains. Peru is the land of the giants from the stars, and if you had a dream of this incredible place, you must go deep into the silence to determine the precise reasons why your guidance has drawn you to the home of the Star Gods.

POCAHONTAS The story of how Pocahontas, the daughter of the powerful chief Powhatan, threw herself over the bound body of Captain John Smith and saved his life at the risk of her own has become one of the most enduring tales of America's early colonial period. Although many may believe the story to be no more than a bit of romantic folklore of a "Romeo and Juliet" frontier style, there really was an Indian woman named Pocahontas who was the daughter of Powhatan, leader of a confederacy of tribes that bore his own name, and she did convince her father to spare the representative of the Virginia colony. Although there was no subsequent romance between Captain Smith and his lovely savior, the act of selflessness on her part led to improved relationships between the Powhatans, and the august chief became a friend of the settlers.

About 1609, Captain Smith returned to England, leaving his friends among the colonists and the Powhatans, and also leaving Jamestown in a much improved condition than it was upon his arrival.

In the wake of increased contact with the settlers, Pocahontas became a Christian and was renamed Lady Rebecca. In 1612 she met John Rolfe in Jamestown; and in April of 1613, they were married. In 1616, the Rolfes traveled to England where the charming Pocahontas was presented at court and received warmly by the assembly. Sadly, a year later, during an outbreak of smallpox, she succumbed to the disease and died. The Rolfes' one son, Thomas, eventually returned to Virginia where he became a prosperous man.

If you feel intuitively that you have somehow received thoughts, images, or messages from the spirit energy of Pocahontas, you should prepare yourself to go as deep as possible into the silence in order to determine the reasons why you have been chosen for such contact. You may have been touched by the spirit of Pocahontas in order to alert your consciousness to the true mission that you chose to come to the planet to accomplish.

PONTIAC Born around 1720 in what is now Ohio, Pontiac became the greatest of the Ottawa chiefs and one of the most brilliant military strategists of the Indian people. Although he surrendered to Major Robert Rogers in 1760 in a place now known as Cleveland and turned over Detroit to the British, he soon became dissatisfied with the cavalier treatment afforded his people by the redcoats. Pontiac had acquiesced and signed the treaty only to prevent continued attacks by the British upon the Ottawas; but when, aghast, he saw the ill treatment that his tribe received from the redcoats as a conquered nation under their rule, he decided that the rigors of battle and the trials of the warpath were better for his people than suppression and subjugation.

The power of his charisma united all of the tribes northwest of the Ohio River, and he led his mighty army against all of the British forts and outposts on the Great Lakes. Humiliated by the "savages" who descended upon them, the British lost all but two of their ten forts. Only Detroit and Fort Pitt managed to hold out against the determined warriors that Pontiac had assembled to humble the red coats who had so cruelly dealt with his people.

Finally, on August 17, 1769, the indefatigable war chief made peace with his enemies at Detroit, thereby reinstating the terms that he had outlined fifteen years before. In 1769, Pontiac was struck down and murdered by one of his own people.

If you feel that you have received thoughts, images, and inspirations that are somehow associated with the spirit energy of the great Pontiac, you should undergo a brief period of fasting before you allow yourself to go deep into the silence of meditation and seek to determine more precisely the reasons why you have been selected for such a contact from the spirit world. You may have been contacted to order to activate a higher level of your consciousness to begin a more active pursuit of the goals which you incarnated on earth to accomplish.

RABBIT Many of the eastern tribes revered the spirit entity of the Great Rabbit as a sacred teacher of skills, arts, and crafts--and even as a participant with the Great Mystery in the creation of humankind. Undoubtedly the rabbit's well known attributes of fertility and reproduction were related to action, life, and growth. Its large red eyes were representative of the living fire of blood and the life force that courses through every living creature. Its ability to change its gray coat to white in its winter transfiguration was likely associated in the Indians' mind with the change from rain to snow and thus allied the rabbit with the spirits of thunder and storm. Its nimble and quick actions, its flying leaps, connected the rabbit to the mystery of unfettered upward movement shared with the birds and the trees. Even the name of the Iroquois' legendary culture bearer Manabozho is derived from the words for "great" and for "rabbit."

Grandmother Twylah of the Seneca says that the symbol of a rabbit that looks to the west with one eye shut to its immediate surroundings indicates that one has a disregard for the future.

To dream of a rabbit with its ears upright is to be reminded that one should listen intensely to what is truly being said in one's presence.

According to Grandmother, the symbol of the rabbit generally means that a person is always ready to handle sudden challenges--but that he or she sometimes acts before fully evaluating the true nature of the challenge.

A rabbit that looks to the north, Grandmother says, is a symbol of the input of wisdom. Looking to the south reveals egotistical tendencies; to the east, the wish to seek friends.

Pictoglyph of the
Great Rabbit.

If you have dreamed of sighting many rabbits on the run, your guide is informing you that your coming business ventures should prove successful.

A dream scenario in which you have shot a rabbit indicates happiness. If you proceeded to eat the rabbit, however, you will soon quarrel with a friend.

Should your personal visions have revealed the rabbit as your totem animal then its appearance in any of your dreams will have the express purpose of alerting you to take careful note of a series of important symbols that your guide will cause to follow. These symbols will be designed to assist you in making important decisions in your life, so you must ponder each of them in order to interpret correctly their precise meaning and application in the balanced walking of your path.

RAINBOW The Nevada Indians believe that the rainbow is a serpent, whose shining scales are its colors. A legend of certain of the eastern tribes has it that when a soul wishes to descend to the Earth Mother to enter a human body, a mouse must scurry up to a rainbow and gnaw a hole in its colorful threads to permit the spirit to enter. The California Indians maintain that the rainbow is the sister of the Great Creator Spirit, who wears many beautiful flowers upon her breast.

To dream of a rainbow is to receive a symbol of good health and prosperity.

If you dreamt of seeing a rainbow together with your lover or spouse, you will have a long and agreeable relationship.

A dream in which you saw a rainbow arching directly over your head is likely a symbol from your guide indicating a family inheritance coming your way.

If you had a time sense in your night vision, a rainbow seen at sunrise is a symbol of great riches about to be yours. A rainbow viewed at sunset represents good times ahead.

RED CLOUD An Ogallala Teton Sioux, Red Cloud was
born along the Platte River in Nebraska around 1822. As a
chief concerned for the good of his people, Red Cloud went
to war only in an effort to guard the dwindling source of the
Plains Indians' principal food source, the buffalo.

Although he would not have had such statistics at his
disposal, at the time of Red Cloud's birth there were an
estimated 60 million buffalo on the Plains. When he began
his war to preserve the buffalo in 1865, their numbers had
decreased to an estimated 13 million.

Red Cloud was aware that the great slaughter of the
buffalo began in bloody earnest in the 1860s with the
building of the railroad lines across the Plains. Hunters
who were employed to keep the crews in meat began to
kill the great animals in ever-increasing numbers. In
1866, when Red Cloud learned of a new plan to make a
road along the Bozeman Trail to service the goldfields
of Montana, he declared all-out war. Although his
raiding parties had already terrorized Dakota territory,
his full-scale war parties soon caused the trail to be called
"the Bloody Bozeman."

Captain William J. Fetterman arrived at Fort Phil
Kearney and uttered the famous, ill-fated boast that
expressed his well-known contempt for the Indian.
Give him but 80 men, he sneered, and he would be able
to ride through the entire Sioux nation.

When Red Cloud learned of the insulting bravado, he
decided to give the Pony Soldier his wish. Drawing
Fetterman and his prescribed 80 men outside of the fort
with an attack on the woodcutters, Red Cloud's warriors taunted the bold officer into pursuit. Within a
matter of a few gory minutes, Fetterman and his requi-
site eighty troopers were annihilated by Red Cloud's
defiant warriors.

In 1868, the government decided to abandon Fort Phil
Kearney. Red Cloud rode in triumph through the hated
walls, then burned it to the ground. Shortly thereafter,
he surrendered to the inevitable relentless rush of the

white man's soldiers, railroads, and settlements, but he did so with the air of a victor who had won what he had set out to achieve--the preservation of the buffalo hunting grounds for his people.

Sadly, Red Cloud's victory was short-lived. By then, buffalo slaughter had become a sport for eastern gentlemen. At the time of his death in 1909, the number of buffalo in the United States was estimated to be fewer than 1,000.

If it is your belief that you have received thoughts, images, and messages from the spirit energy of the great Red Cloud, you should undergo a brief fast before you enter the silence to go deep into other dimensions of being to determine the reasons why you have been chosen for such a spiritual alignment. You may have been contacted by such a powerful vibration in order to activate your higher self to assist you in understanding the true purpose for your having come to the earth plane in your present incarnation.

RED JACKET Our Grandmother Twylah is a direct descendant of the great Seneca orator and chief, Red Jacket. Born about 1756 at Canoga, New York, he fought on the side of the Crown during the Revolution, thus gaining his name from the many bright red coats that the British awarded him.

Red Jacket and the Seneca people stood fast by Medicine Power and the old traditions and resented very much the intrusion of the black-coated missionaries on the reservation. Once, after bearing patiently an impassioned missionary's fire-and-brimstone sermon, Red Jacket told him, "If you white people murdered the 'savior,' you must make up for it. We had nothing to do with it. If he had come among us, we should have treated him better."

Around the year 1821, a missionary from Massachusetts petitioned the Seneca to hold a council at Buffalo, New York. The Black Coat insisted that he did not wish the Seneca's land or their money, he only wanted them to accept the one true God – and he demanded that he receive an

The Great Mystery.

answer from the tribe before he left them. Herewith are excerpts from Red Jacket's masterful reply:

"Friend and Brother! It was the will of the Great Spirit that we should meet together this day...and he has given us a fine day for our council. Brother! This council fire was kindled by you. It was at your request that we came together at this time. We have listened with attention to what you have said. You requested us to speak our minds freely. This gives us great joy...All have heard your voice, and all speak to you as one man...

"...There was a time when our forefathers owned this great island...The Great Spirit made it for the use of Indians. He had created the buffalo, the deer, and other animals for food...He had caused the earth to produce corn for bread. All this he had done for his red children because he loved them....

"...But an evil day came upon us. Your forefathers crossed the great waters and landed on this island...They found friends and not enemies...We gave them corn and meat. They gave us poison in return...

"...At length their numbers increased greatly. They wanted more land. They wanted our country...Wars took place. Indians were hired to fight against Indians, and many of our people were destroyed....

"...Brother! Our lands were once large, and yours were very small. You have now become a great people, and we have scarcely a place left to spread our blankets. But still you are not satisfied. You now want to force your religion upon us...You say that you are right and we are lost. How do we know this to be true?...How shall we know what to believe, being so often deceived by the white people?

"Brother! You say there is but one way to worship and serve the Great Spirit. If there is but one religion, why do you white people differ so much about it? Why do you not all agree, as you can all read the book?

"...We also have a religion that was given to our forefathers and has been handed down to us, their children...It teaches us to be thankful for all the favors we receive, to love each other, and to be united. We never quarrel about religion....We do not wish to destroy your religion or take it from you. We only want to enjoy our own.

"...We are told that you have been preaching to the white people in [Buffalo]. These people are our neighbors...We will wait a little while and see what effect your preaching has upon them. If we find that it does them good and makes them honest and less disposed to cheat Indians, we will then consider again what you have said.

"You have now heard our answer to your talk, and this is all we have to say at present. As we are going to part, we will take you by the hand and hope the Great Spirit will protect you and return you safe to your friends."

Although Red Jacket came forward to shake hands at this, the conclusion of his remarks, the Black Coat turned his back on the chief and refused the handshake offered in tolerant friendship.

In 1824, Red Jacket achieved the victory of having the mission of the Black Coats removed from the Seneca reservation. The brilliant orator and accomplished military leader died in Buffalo on January 20, 1830.

If you believe that you have received thoughts, images, and messages from the spirit energy of the great Red Jacket, you should undergo a brief period of fasting before you prepare yourself to go deep into the silence to learn the exact reasons why you have been contacted by such a powerful vibration. Carefully analyze the symbols that have been given to you by this spirit energy and understand that you may be told that you are to perform acts of meaningful service to the Earth Mother and all of her children.

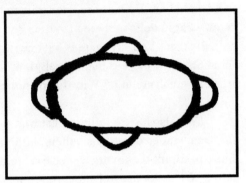

The Breath Master,
Giver of Life.

SACAJAWEA A Shoshone woman who had been captured by the Mandan of North Dakota when she was fourteen, Sacajawea acted as interpreter for Lewis and Clark on their history-making Corps of Discovery expedition in 1804-06. In exchange for her services, the explorers promised to return her to her tribe in the Rocky Mountains.

A woman of obvious intellect and many talents, Sacajawea proved invaluable to the explorers as they encountered new tribes, as well as nearly ceaseless natural hazards, on their wilderness trek. In addition to assuming a role on the expedition which required great courage and physical endurance, Sacajawea also gave birth to a son while on the trip.

Surviving to a hardy old age, she died near Fort Washakie, Wyoming, on April 9, 1884. Two statues have been erected to honor the memory of Sacajawea-- one in Portland, Oregon; another in Bismarck, North Dakota.

If you believe that you have received thoughts, images, or inspiration from the spirit energy of this remarkably courageous entity, you should prepare yourself to go deep into the silence to understand better why you have been contacted by the vibrations of the great Sacajawea. This communication may have been established in order to alert your higher consciousness to the true mission that you chose to come to the planet to fulfill.

SCORPION A night vision which places you before a nest of scorpions is offering you a warning that enemies are talking about you behind your back. If a single scorpion leaves the nest and begins to move toward you, you should be prepared to undergo some damages to your business or personal life caused by your enemies.

If you have experienced a dream drama in which you were bitten by a scorpion, you will succeed in your goals.

If you have dreamed of killing a scorpion, you will suffer losses through the ministrations of false friends.

SEA If your guide has given you a dream in which you have stood on the beach watching small waves rolling in from the open sea, you have been offered a foreshadowing of good fortune of generous proportions coming your way. If the waves should grow suddenly larger, you may expect help from the unseen world in achieving spiritual, as well as, physical goals.

A dream which depicts you as falling into the sea is providing you with a warning that you should be cautious of the jealousy of certain close friends. If, after you have fallen, you manage to grab onto some object floating in the water which can support you, you will be able to overcome their jealousy and maintain their true friendship.

If you have been presented with a dream drama in which you are traveling across a very smooth sea, you have been given a symbol of devoted love within your family.

A night vision in which you and your spouse or significant other are being buffeted about by a rough sea and stormy winds indicates that you will be blessed with a great and lasting love.

If you have seen yourself in a dream in which you were

bathing in a dirty, contaminated sea, your earnest striving toward a particular goal will be only meagerly rewarded. If you were bathing in a clear, blue sea, the problems in achieving that goal will be conquered. If you were to be suddenly joined by a number of men and women bathers, you will likely achieve the goal, but receive more honor than profit.

SEATTLE In 1890, the people of Seattle, Washington, erected a monument over the grave of a chief who had always remained their friend--in spite of the many unconscionable acts worked against him. Born about 1790 in the area around Puget Sound, Chief Seathe (Seattle) uttered this prophetic admonition to the whitemen who had cheated his people out of their lands with the Treaty of Point Elliott in 1855:

"...Our religion is the traditions of our ancestors, the dreams of our old men, given them by the Great Spirit, and the visions of our shamans, and is written in the hearts of our people....

"Every part of this country is sacred to my people. Every hillside, every valley, every plain and grove has been hallowed by some fond memory or some sad experience of my tribe....

"The braves, loving mothers, glad-hearted maidens, and even little children, who lived there...still love these solitudes. Their deep fastnesses at eventide grow shadowy with the presence of dusty spirits.

"When the last red man shall have perished from the earth and his memory among the white men shall have become a myth, these shores shall swarm with the invisible dead of my tribe...

"At night when the streets of your cities and villages shall be silent, and you think them deserted, they will throng with the returning hosts that once filled and still love this beautiful land.

"The white man will never be alone. Let him be just and deal kindly with my people, for the dead are not altogether powerless. 'Dead,' did I say? There is no death, only a change of worlds.

If in the quiet of your reverie you believe that you have

received thoughts, images, inspirations, and messages that you feel might have somehow issued from the spirit energy of the great Seattle, you should begin a process of self-examination before you enter the silence to determine the precise reasons for such powerful vibrations having come into your life. Contact from such a source as the spirit energy of Seattle may serve as guidance in alerting you to your true mission in life.

SEED If your guide has given you a dream in which you saw yourself walking with a bag of seeds over your shoulder, there is a marriage in the offing for you or a close friend or relative.

If you perceived yourself planting seeds in an area that you had tilled, you have viewed a symbol of approaching good fortune. If the seeds you planted were those of vegetables, you will undergo some discomfort before your success arrives. If the seeds were those of flowers, there will be much pain accompanying the attainment of your goal.

Should your dream scenario have depicted you setting out to plant a field, but finding seed only fit to feed birds, you may soon face a situation that will bring your dishonor.

SERPENT Father Charlevoix, an early French "Black Robe," remarked that there was no creature that the Indian tribes marked upon their faces and other parts of their bodies more than that of the serpent. Furthermore, according to the priest's observations, "...they have the secret of charming (snakes)...of benumbing them...so that they take them alive, handle them, and put them in their bosom without receiving any hurt."

The rattlesnake was considered the chief of all serpents; and some tribes believed that in addition to delivering death via the strike of its deadly fangs, the rattler could transmit diseases with a glance of its beady eyes.

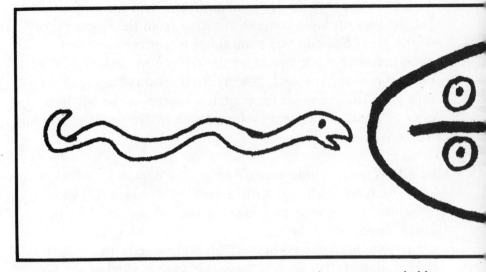

Symbol of the Life Force. In this instance, the serpents probably represent fire; the oval, an egg; and the four circles above and below the line, the power of the four winds that move the sky and the Earth Mother.

If a coiled rattlesnake should manifest in the path of a warrior, he would freeze in his tracks, speak beseechingly to it, and offer it whatever gifts he had on his person that he hoped might appease the angry rattler. A chant that proposed peace between the serpent and the children of men was always ready on the lips of those who spent any amount of time away from the village.

The Medicine Priests who walked among the rattle-snakes knew that the powerful essence of the Great Mystery moved through them. The shaman revered the serpent for its great wisdom, and many believed that the snake spoke a secret language of its own that no other animal was permitted to comprehend. According to many tribal legends, in the beginning of life on the Earth Mother, humans and snakes could converse freely. If one were powerfully attuned on the spirit level, the Medicine Priests believed, telepathic communication could still exist between human and snake, and the secrets of the future and other arcane knowledge could be derived from a mindlink with a serpent.

The skin of the rattlesnake was used by nearly all Medicine Priests in some aspect of their rituals, and

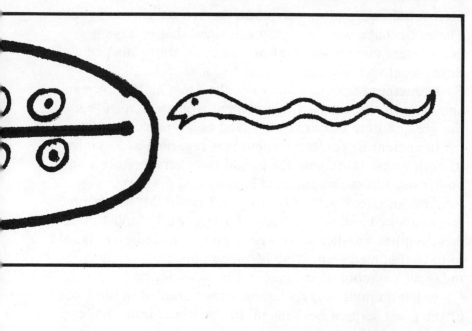

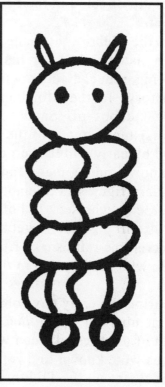

A feminine Moon spirit, perhaps of negative intent, since she also wears the coils of a serpent.

their rattles were often carried in the priests' sacred pouches. The rattlesnake was so highly esteemed that to have it as one's totem elevated a chief or a shaman above his peers. Some went so far as to claim reptilian ancestors.

In ancient Mexico, *Ciuacoatl*, the great mother of men and gods, is represented as a serpent woman. *Quetza-coatl*, the great culture bearer, is depicted as a winged serpent.

In ancient Egypt, the serpent was regarded as a symbol of both immortality and death, and the pharaoh wore a snake on his headdress as a mark of royalty and divinity.

Apollo, Greek god of healing and medicine, was originally invoked and worshipped as a serpent. In later times, Aesculapius, another deity associated with medicine, is said to have assumed serpentine form, and his crest remains today as a symbol of the medical profession.

In Hindu mythology, Vishnu sleeps cradled in the folds of the great serpent Seshanaga. In the Hindu tradition, evil spirits are directed in their misdeeds by their leader, a great serpent.

In the Hebrew account of the fall from Paradise, the serpent is punished for his part in the seduction of Eve by being reduced to crawling on his belly for the rest of history. In the Mohammedan tradition, the angel Michael chops off Satan's legs with the sword of God.

Persistent legends of the Serpent People who had to be bested by early culture heroes of the East and Mid-East are also known among many Indian tribes, who depict such legendary figures as Manabozho battling, and conquering, the serpents who seek to hold humankind in bondage.

It is still possible to get some of the elders to speak of the incredible rattlesnake ritual of the Yokut tribe, the people who used to live in the San Joaquin Valley of California.

During the early days of spring, a Yokut shaman would lead members of the *Tiidum* snake cult in a march to the mouth of a rattlesnake den where the largest of the deadly reptiles were known to dwell. Once assembled in formation before the cave, the Tiidum began a whistling, foot-stamp-

An ancient pictoglyph
which represents the old
legend that in the primeval
world, humans and snakes
could converse freely with
one another.

ing, chanting cacophony that was orchestrated to wake the snakes from their winter slumber.

After a time, the angered rattlers would appear, writhing their way directly toward the shaman and the cultists who had so rudely terminated their hibernation. With practiced motions, the shaman distracted the giant rattlers so cult members could snatch them up and place them in a large woven bag.

When a good number of the furiously twisting rattlers had been collected, the Medicine priest returned to the village and placed the sacked serpents above the head of each member of the Yokut community. By observing certain signs, the sacred priest could foresee which of the villagers would fall victim to the poisonous fangs of a rattlesnake in the year to come. When such an omen was apparent, the Medicine priest practiced a ritual cure upon the potential victim that was very much the same as the procedure to treat an actual snake bite.

The Yokut believed that when a person was bitten by a snake, a serpentine essence entered the body along with the venom and that no cure could be effective unless the reptilian invader was sucked out along with the poison. Using a heated stone applied over the wound, the Medicine priest sucked out the poison brought to the surface, then produced a small snake from his mouth, presumably a representation of the one that had pierced the victim's flesh along with the injected venom.

Once such demonstrations of their power over the rattlesnake had been displayed, the shaman and the snake cult dug a pit and filled it with hundreds of deadly rattlesnakes. With the necessary invocations to protect themselves from the serpents, the cult members stepped to the edge of the pit where the rattlers were fighting the slopes of their confinement, angrily lashing upward with their deadly fangs.

Calmly, the shaman bent his head to stare deeply into the churning mass of snakes. Then, in a blur of motion, his hand flashed into the pit and snatched a massive rattlesnake free from the writhing bodies of its brothers.

With a sudden shake of his powerful wrist, the Yokut Medicine priest threw the rattler upward, as if to give it a home in the sky. Seemingly impassive, almost indifferent, the shaman watched the twisting body spin through the air, then caught it just before the furious snake struck the ground. With another seemingly disdainful movement, the priest tossed the snake back into the pit.

Taking their cue from the shaman, members of the *Tiidum* began to pick up arm-thick rattlers with complete unconcern. Dozens of the snakes were thrown high into the air, then caught again by the fearless cult members. Some cultists became so adept at snake tossing that they would coolly step under the fall of maddened rattlers and let them drop around their bare shoulders.

The Tiidum ritual often drove the rattlers to such frenzy that they bit themselves or other nearby snakes in their wild need to strike out at whatever was so ruthlessly violating their sovereignty.

Some Yokut Medicine priests became so practiced at handling serpents that they were able to place the rattlers' fangs on the tips of their fingers and hold the snake at arm's length without the reptiles being able to close their jaws for a satisfying bite.

The Yokut shamans' heart-stopping game of catch with the rattlesnake was only a warm-up for the sacred ritual that the whole tribe would perform on the next day. The Tiidum, the Yokut snake cult, would lead the tribe in the ancient *Datlawash* ceremonies, designed to protect the people from the deadly bite of the rattler, with whom they shared their Southwestern home.

That night in the Yokut village, aged women to whom alone the sacred songs were entrusted, made their way through the camp by torchlight, singing eerie, timeless chants that would keep homes safe from fatal intrusion by snakes.

At dawn the snake shamans led the tribe in the Datlawash, the "stepping-over" ceremony in which each Yokut, from the very youngest to the most aged, walked to the rim of the deadly pit of rattlesnakes and passed his or her right foot over the writhing reptilian mass just scant inches below. The Datlawash would endow the Yokut with a life-saving advantage during the coming year: no rattlesnake would strike without first shaking his tail to provide a warning.

Grandmother Twylah of the Seneca says that a snake represents wisdom. The snake attacks only when it is provoked or challenged--a trait common to people who have the ability to develop their inner-knowing.

Should your visions have revealed the snake as your totem animal, its appearance in any of your dreams will alert you to take careful notice of a series of important symbols that will be certain to follow. A careful analysis of these signs will be certain to provide you with valuable insights in solving any problem that might be vexing you.

A dream of a snake coiling around your body is warning you of deceitful and ungrateful people near you.

If you have seen a many-headed serpent in your dream, you must be on guard against enemies in both the seen and unseen worlds. If you physically struggle with the serpent and slay it, you will achieve victory over your enemies. If you were unable to kill the snake, your enemies are better prepared in their attack against you than you anticipated.

A dream in which you are bitten by a snake is a message from your guide advising you that your enemies are accusing you of evil deeds.

If your night vision depicts you encountering a snake that is coiled and ready to strike, you are being alerted to the treachery of someone whom you would least expect of betrayal.

A dream scenario which portrays you traveling with a snake in a cage is presenting you with a positive symbol of your winning success after taking a desperate gamble.

SEQUOYA The redwoods in California were named after this remarkable Cherokee genius as a fitting memorial to the man who developed an alphabet for his people. Born in Taskigi, Tennessee, about 1760, Sequoya (also spelled Sequoia) perceived that the whiteman received great power from his ability to read and to write. Although he began not understanding a single letter, he told his chiefs that he would create an alphabet for the Cherokee nation.

The tribal council scoffed, reminding Sequoya that the Great Mystery had given a book to the whiteman, a bow and arrow to the redman. Therefore, they argued, a redman could not make a book.

Sequoya went into seclusion to study. His corn went to weeds, and everyone analyzed his behavior as that of a crazy man. His unsympathetic wife burned his manuscripts whenever she found them.

At last, in 1821, he had isolated the sixty-eight "sounds" of the Cherokee language and adopted a character for each one; and these characters, combined like letters, form words. In 1828, the first Indian newspaper, the *Cherokee Phoenix*, was printed, an event "sacred to the cause of the Indian."

If you believe that you have been receiving thoughts, images, and inspiration from the spirit energy of the great Sequoya, you should undergo a process of self-examination designed to prepare you to enter the silence in an effective manner. Analyze any symbols which may be revealed to you that will explain why you have been contacted by this powerful vibration from the dimension of spirit. Quite likely the transmissions will have a great deal to do with your true mission on the Earth Mother.

SITTING BULL Perhaps the most controversial personality in the long and bloody history of the Indian wars was the dynamic Sioux chief and medicine man known to the white man's history as Sitting Bull. Born about 1834 in South Dakota, the future leader of the Hunkpapa Teton Sioux had the name Jumping Badger. Later, after a battle with the white soldiers in 1857, his medicine told him to assume the name of Sitting Bull.

An army major who had encountered the war chief said that he was possessed of an evil face and shifty eyes. Sitting Bull, he stated, was crafty, greedy, ambitious, and a physical coward.

Wooden Leg, a Cheyenne warrior, said that he would

Zuni hunting shield. Notice the lines on the bear and the eagle moving from head to heart. The drawing of the prey's heart was a method designed to give the hunter mastery over their lifeforce.

not hear of anyone questioning the courage of Sitting Bull. According to this comrade-at-arms, Sitting Bull was a brave man with a "big brain and a good one."

In his own defense, Sitting Bull once asked, "What white man can say I ever stole his lands or a penny of his money?...What white woman...was ever, when a captive, insulted by me?...What white man has ever seen me drunk? Who has ever come to me hungry and gone unfed? Who has ever seen me beat my wives or abuse my children?...[Am I] wicked because my skin is red; because I am a Sioux; because I was born where my fathers lived; because I would die for my people and my country?"

Sitting Bull predicted that he would conquer Custer at the Little Big Horn; and after the Indians' victory on June 25, 1876, his medicine, always revered by the Sioux, gained even greater respect among other Plains tribes.

After Custer's defeat, Sitting Bull and his people crossed the border to Canada. About a year after the battle on the Little Big Horn, he explained his reasons why the Indians fought Yellow Hair to Canadian journalists: "I was driven in force from my land. I never made war on the United States Government...The white man came on my land and followed me. The white man made me fight for my own hunting grounds. The white man made me kill him or he would kill my friends, my women, and my children.

"...We did not know Custer...I did not want to kill any more men. I did not like that kind of work. I only defended my camp. When we had killed enough, that was all that was necessary."

In 1881, Sitting Bull surrendered to the U.S. army and was confined at Fort Randall until 1883. Upon his release, he was hired by Buffalo Bill to join his famous touring Wild West Show, and interestingly enough, he became a very popular figure throughout the United States and Europe.

Around 1888, Sitting Bull became intrigued by the vision of Wovoka and his Ghost Dance religion. Inspired by the promise of a new age when the buffalo would return and the

white man would be driven from tribal lands, the Sioux
began to put on the ghost shirts and to dance back the spirits
of the old traditions.

In December of 1890, Sitting Bull, who had become
an impassioned leader of the new religion, was murdered
"while resisting arrest."

If you have become convinced that you have been
receiving thoughts, images, and inspiration from the
spirit energy of the great Sitting Bull, you should undergo a process of self-evaluation and self-discipline
before you enter the silence of deep meditation and
determine the exact reasons why such a powerful vibration from the dimension of spirit has made contact with
you. You should likely prepare yourself to be of meaningful service to the Earth Mother and all of her children, for communication with such a forceful entity as
Sitting Bull will undoubtedly concern itself with your
true mission on the planet.

SPIDER   The Cherokee have a folktale in which the
spider answered humankind's prayer for fire and brought
the mystic energy on its gossamer web from the Spirit
of Flame to the tribes of America.

An unmarried person who dreams of a spider will
soon be making wedding plans. A married person who
has encountered a spider in his or her dream scenario and
who has been bitten by it will soon be faced with
evidence of marital unfaithfulness.

To dream of watching a spider spinning a web is to
receive a symbol of domestic happiness.

If your guide has created a dream scenario in which
you discover a spider crawling on your body you are
bound to receive good fortune just ahead. If such a discovery was made in a night time dream setting, you may expect
a great deal of money. If you found the spider in a morning
time dream drama, there may be a lawsuit that will encum-
ber your good fortune.

STAR In the cosmology of most traditional Medicine Priests, the stars moved across the skies propelled by their own indwelling power. The larger stars, they believed, were appointed by the Great Mystery as guardians of the smaller ones. Clusters of stars were thought to be cities; constellations were considered the council-gathering of spirit beings.

Most tribes believed that the stars were the dwelling places of spirit entities who had a personal relationship to human souls. Both the hieroglyphs of the ancient Egyptians and the pictoglyphs of the American Indians indicate a belief that the stars housed ministering spirits that exerted a great influence on the lives of those who walked on the Earth Mother.

Such tribes as the Chippewa maintained that star beings visited the villages from time to time and took of themselves human wives and husbands. Hunters coming upon peculiar circles in the prairies or in forest clearings believed the marks to have been made by the Star People coming to earth in large baskets. According

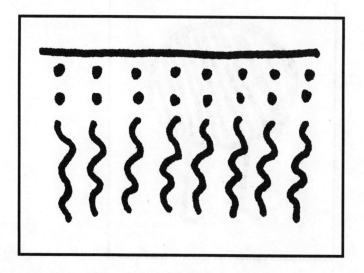

The two lines of dots in the upper portion of this pictoglyph suggest the multitude of stars in the night sky. The wavy lines beneath each star indicates the Indian belief that rays from the stars could exert an influence upon their lives. Each star had a personal will which was directed by the Great Mystery and was concerned with individuals on their earthwalk.

to the old legends, warriors might well fall in love with these Daughters of the Stars; but on occasion, Sons of the Stars were not above kidnapping a daughter of the tribes.

To dream of viewing a sky full of shooting stars is to receive a symbol from your guide that certain troubles that have been bothering you on your life path are about to disappear.

If you have seen yourself in a dream scenario looking up at a night sky filled with stars, you are walking in good balance and may expect continued happiness. If the stars suddenly became a bit dim, your guide is warning you not to place a great deal of confidence in others.

If one star should become brighter than all the others, you have been given a sign of approaching losses in your business affairs. If all the stars begin to move from being rather dim to being very bright, you will be able to overcome the losses and graduate to prosperity.

A Star Spirit

A night vision in which the light of a particular star appears to shine directly into your room is foreshadowing the death of a close relative.

If you have dreamed of a star that fell upon your house, you should brace yourself for the discovery that your lover has been unfaithful.

Old European symbol of the spirit (a dove) soaring from a mountain top (illumination) to a star (higher consciousness).

STORM If your guide has fashioned a dream drama of a violent storm, you must be prepared for the bad news that certain of your business goals have been demolished.

A dream which has you observing the approach of a storm has given you a sign of dark clouds forming in your love relationship. If the storm should catch you outdoors in your dream, you are being warned of a coming separation from your loved one.

If you have experienced a dream in which a storm struck your home but effected little damage, your guide is advising you that you are about to discover an important secret. If the storm damaged your home to some degree, but, basically, it remained solid, you have been shown a symbol of your good morals allowing you to overcome personal attacks by your enemies. If the storm managed to destroy your home, you must strenuously guard against the evil intentions of hidden enemies along your life path.

SUN The Cherokee have a legend that tells of the Great
Mystery creating the Earth Mother and deciding that all
humans should be immortal. The Sun, however, surveyed the
prairies, forests, and streams and estimated that the land
could not support a prolific immortal humanity. Death, he
decreed, must re-enter the program. But when his daughter
was bitten by a serpent and became the first to die, the Sun
decided to review the Great Mystery's original plan. He
commissioned a few trusted humans to capture his
daughter's spirit in a box where it might be carefully sheltered. Once her spirit was safe, the Sun announced that men
and women should live forever--as long as the box that
harbored his daughter's spirit was never opened. As fate
would have it, a curious person opened the box, and the
daughter's spirit fled--human immortality with it.

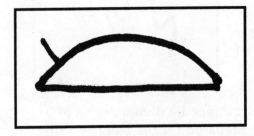

Pictoglyphs for sunrise,
sunset, and fire, the connecting link between the natural
and the supernatural worlds.

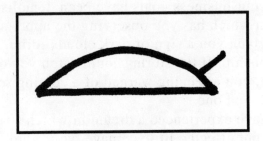

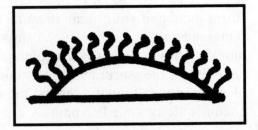

Thus the Cherokee perceived that the sun had a great deal to do with life--and death--on the Earth Mother.

Some tribes believed that the sun was represented by the eagle, which became a greatly venerated bird because of the worshipful association. Some Medicine Priests even maintained that a feather of those particular eagles that seemed to fly directly into the sun could make the bearer invisible and invulnerable.

Numerous rituals were begun with the chief or shaman offering his lighted pipe three times to the rising sun, then guiding it from east to west, all the while praying for the sun to favor the tribe.

Among the Huron, the primary chiefs would rise with the sun, turn themselves toward the east, uttering a cry of supplication three times, then bow down to the earth. After completing this ritual, the chiefs would light their pipes and blow the smoke toward the sun. This step realized, they would next perform the same rite to the four directions.

Many tribes observed particular ceremonies and feasts in celebration of the sun and its life-giving energy. Not all tribes made a clear association between the benevolent rays of the sun and the fecundity of nature, but the cosmology of most Medicine Priests believed that the sun was omnipresent wherever its illumination reached, seeing everything that transpired during the daylight hours. In the

In this pictoglyph the sun is depicted with ears, indicating that not only did the celestial orb see all things, it also listened to every conversation and identified every sound.

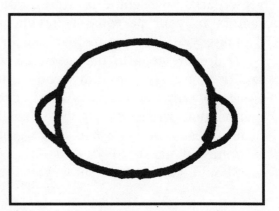

Chippewa dialect, for example, the sun is called He Who Sees Us. Those who received visions of the sun during the various prescribed feasts were believed to have been blessed with psychic abilities, the power to see all things.

Glyphs of the sun etched by certain Medicine Priests portrayed the sun with ears, thereby indicating the celestial orb's ability to hear all, as well as see all. A great dream of the sun during a feast in its honor might enable the dreamer to chant: "I am the living body of the Great Spirit."

The Sundance of the Cheyenne and other Plains Indians is perhaps the most well known of the many celebrations of the sun. Observed during the summer, the ritual usually lasted for eight days and involved the insertion of wooden pegs or eagle claws into the pectoral muscles of the celebrants. Those performing the secret rites might dance around a tall pole for several days and nights, then be hoisted by leather thongs attached to the pegs in their chests to hang above the earth suspended on a tall pole; or in other observances, they might pull heavy objects around the pole by means of the thongs in their flesh. The Kiowa performed the Sundance without the elements of self-torture, and all versions of the ceremony involving bloodshed are prohibited by law today.

A dream which portrayed you basking in the sun has offered you a sign that you will receive good news which will lead to great happiness. If the sun began to grow dark, your guide is urging you to be cautious of factors in your personal behavior pattern which could decrease your success in love and in business affairs.

A dream scenario that depicted you observing a lovely sunset is providing you with a warning that someone will soon give you allegedly important information that will prove to be false. If you dreamed of a beautiful sunrise, you may have greater confidence in the information given to you.

Should your dream show you looking up at an overcast sky, watching the sun peep through the clouds, your luck is about to change for the better. If the partially clouded sun should suddenly become red, you are being advised that an illness will soon touch someone close to you.

If your guide created a night vision in which you watched the eclipse of the sun, you must act with great caution so you will not incur losses in a coming business transaction.

A woman who has dreamed of a beautiful sunset is being told that she will be the mother of a child who will have very good medicine.

TECUMSEH General William Henry Harrison once said of Tecumseh that the great Shawnee chief, in another time, another place, could have founded an empire that would have rivaled those of the Aztecs and the Incas. Born about 1768, Tecumseh may have been the greatest of all Indian leaders. Even his staunchest enemies regarded him as brilliant, capable, and honest.

Together with his brother, Tenskwatawa the prophet, Tecumseh, like Pontiac before him, endeavored to unite the tribes in a defensive confederation. Tenskwatawa preached his vision of a return to the traditional virtues and a restoration of the old values; and the fire of his oratory, combined with Tecumseh's military genius, won the allegiance of the Shawnee and the neighboring tribes. By 1811, the large Indian settlement at the junction of Tippecanoe Creek and the Wabash River was strong enough to be deemed a threat to United States security.

General Harrison met with his brilliant adversary many times in an attempt to avoid what both knew was the inevitability of armed conflict. The U.S military officer was at a loss to provide Tecumseh with adequate responses to his charges of broken promises, illegal treaties, and the stealing of Indian lands from chiefs brought under the influence of whiskey, the whiteman's firewater.

At one meeting between the two warriors, Harrison, in an effort to display courtesy toward Tecumseh, ordered that a chair be brought forward for the chief. When told that his "father," the president of the United States, wished him to be seated like the white officers, Tecumseh seated himself Indian-style on the ground and replied scornfully that the sun was his father, the earth, his mother. "I will repose on her bosom," he concluded.

While Tecumseh was away from Tippecanoe persuading the Creek tribe to join the confederacy, Harrison attacked the settlement that had been left under the command of Tenskwatawa. The prophet and the warriors of Tippecanoe fought valiantly, but the village was burned and Tecumseh's dream of a united Indian nation were scattered among the smoldering ashes.

From the white perspective, however, Tecumseh's adversary, General Harrison, attained such popularity because of his surprise attack on the Indian stronghold that many years later he would parlay his claim as the military leader who destroyed Tippecanoe to become the ninth president of the United States.

During the War of 1812, Tecumseh joined the British in Canada and was awarded the rank of brigadier general. When he learned that General Proctor, his commanding officer, planned to withdraw rather than face the advancing American army under General Harrison, Tecumseh accused the British leader of cowardice. In a speech that begged for courage and support, the disillusioned chief addressed Proctor with such words as the following:

> "When war [against the Americans] was declared, [the king of England] gave us the tomahawk, and [said] that he wanted our assistance and that he would certainly get us our lands back, which the Americans had taken from us. You told us at that time to bring our families to this place [Canada], and we did so. You also promised to take care of them--they should want for nothing, while the men would go and fight the enemy...It made our hearts glad to hear that was your wish....

"...But now [General Proctor], we see you drawing back, and we are sorry to see [you] doing so without seeing the enemy. We must compare [your] conduct to a fat dog, that...when affrighted, drops its tail between its legs and runs off.

"...We wish to remain here and fight our enemy...You have got the arms and ammunition which [the king] sent for his red children. If you have an idea of going away, give them to us...Our lives are in the hands of the Great Spirit. We are determined to defend our lands, and if it be his will, we wish to leave our bones upon them."

General Proctor was quite willing to leave Tecumseh, the Shawnee, and their "bones" to stand against the Americans. On October 15, 1813, just prior to the Battle of the Thames, Tecumseh told his assembled chiefs that he had foreseen his death in the fight that day. His prophecy proved to be correct.

If you have received thoughts, images, and inspiration from a spirit being that you believe to be Tecumseh, you should undergo a program of self-evaluation in order to better determine why this great chief has made contact with your higher self. You should then enter the silence and go deep within so that you might accurately analyze the messages that this powerful vibration is transmitting to you. Quite likely you are being prepared on a higher level of your consciousness to enter a life of service to the Earth Mother and all of her children who sincerely seek unity and the oneness.

TREE A tree lives in balance with nature, Grandmother Twylah has said. Its roots tenderly stretch into the soul of Mother Earth as its rich, green foliage moves toward the endless sky. It shares with all, providing food for some, medicine for others, and lodging places for countless creatures. It enjoys a long work span of many years; and when, at last it becomes aged, it silently bends its weathered arms and returns with its gifts to replenish the earth.

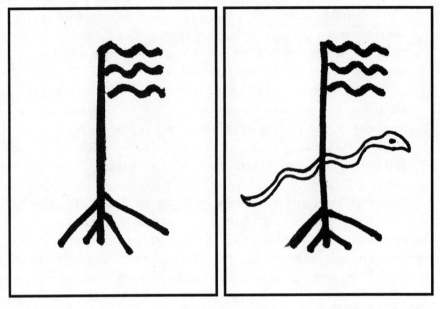

Pictoglyphs depicting (on the
left) a good Medicine tree and a
bad medicine tree.

Grandmother Twylah says that the traditional Seneca
looked to the trees as the examples that guided them toward
personal growth. In her booklet, *Language of the Trees*,
published by the Seneca Indian Historical Society, Twylah
explains how the people of the Iroquois often visited the
forest to commune with their favorite trees. Eventually,
certain trees would come to mean more to them than others,
and they would feel a friendly spirit attracting them. Soon,
that favorite tree would reveal a face, which the Iroquois
would then carve out of the living tree, believing that the
same spirit would remain in the face after the mask was
carved. The trees which yielded the medicine masks were
named Medicine Trees.

To have a vision or a dream which focuses upon the
white pine is to be given a symbol of spiritual expression. The Iroquois found that the white pine provided
them with the wholistic ideal which they could appre-
ciate. The white pine served them spiritually, symboli-
cally, and medicinally. "The shape of the pine tree,"

Grandmother says, "is the image of Truth as it rises to the sky."

A maple tree offers a symbol of giving. Grandmother observes that "maple people" are giving people, just like the tree. Those who choose the maple as a "centering tree" are able to endure hardships, to withstand strong opposition, and still remain true to their convictions.

If you are attracted to the willow tree or have experienced a dream which placed you near one, Grandmother Twylah might say that you are flexible in nature and are easy to live with because of your friendliness. Called the Whispering One by the Seneca, the willow tree is a symbol of people who listen and are soft spoken--people who are excellent thinkers and good friends.

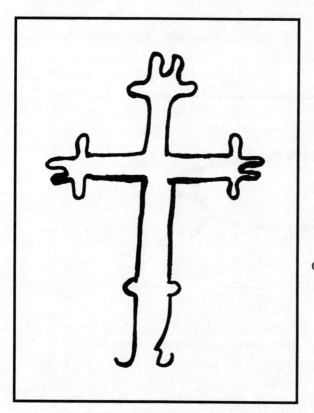

Woden, the Norse All-Father, hung as a sacrifice for nine days on the tree Iggsdrasil. The Christian sings hymns of Christ suffering and dying on a tree. This interesting symbol shows a blending of the ancient tradition of the Tree of Life and the cross.

If your centering tree is the oak, you are quite likely, a solid, dependable, self-disciplined person. Grandmother Twylah would say that you might not be very adventurous, but you have high ideals and are always seeking new mental horizons to conquer. You are also blessed with the gift of foresight, and you do not hesitate to support worthy causes.

People who choose an apple tree as their centering tree have the knack for attracting good, healthy attitudes into their lives. If you found yourself near an apple tree in a dream, your guide provided you with a symbol of dependability and sincerity. You are quite likely a leader among your peers because of your principles and your code of honor.

Grandmother Twylah has observed that people who are drawn to birch trees are supportive individuals who make close friends and who most often enter service-oriented professions. The white birch is also a medicinal tree, whose bark and twigs yield healing and healthful teas; and birch people make excellent doctors, teachers, and spiritual advisors.

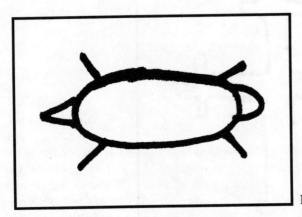

Pictoglyph of a turtle.

TURTLE The world that the Indian tribes knew existed on the back of a great turtle. North America, Canada, and Mexico constitute that land mass that the traditional Indian refers to as Turtle Island.

The Turtle Clan is the peace clan in the earthwalk that comprises the circle of village life. Grandmother

Twylah explains that to the Seneca the turtle is the creature of peace and the symbol of peace. "The turtle rattle is emblematic of peace of mind, and it is used in the dances to help portray happiness. Peace is a state of mind. It can be attained through daily learning experiences. We must learn and understand how to walk in balance on the Pathway of Peace."

The Grandfather of Humans on the
back of Turtle Island, North America

If you have dreamt of the powerful Medicine symbol of the turtle, you have been given a sign by your guide that a great opportunity is about to open up for you.

If your dream scenario featured you buying a number of turtles, you are being advised to evaluate your life style more carefully so that you will better balance your walk on the path.

A dream in which you are cooking turtles in a large pot provided you with a symbol that wealth and influence will be yours if you exercise caution on your earthwalk. If the dream scenario progressed to the point where you were eating the soup made of the turtles, you will likely to enjoy long life and success.

If your dream depicted you in a boat on the ocean observing a large sea turtle, you may expect a change of luck for the better. If you went on to capture the sea turtle, you will soon solve a problem that has long proved to be a mystery for you. If you ate the sea turtle, your guide has given you a sign that you must be alerted to secret enemies around you.

If your visions and quest have revealed the turtle as your totem animal then its appearance in any of your dreams will signal you to take careful notice of a series of important symbols that will be certain to follow its manifestation in the night vision. These symbols have been designed by your guide to provide you with vital clues that will aid you in making the right decisions in any matters that may be troubling you. Analyze them with the utmost of care.

Brad Steiger stands in the tomb in Machu Piccu that tradition
designates as the final resting place of Viracocha.

Viracocha

Viracocha, the great emperor of the massive Inca
empire, was known as a mystic whose dreams regularly
foretold the future. Even as a youth, his reputation as a
seer complemented the respect that he received as a
prince of royal Incan blood.

While he was yet a young man, he foretold insurrec-
tions among several northern tribes. Though his father,
the king, was doubtful that the people he believed to

be loyal could possibly be planning revolt against his rule, he had seen enough of Viracocha's seership to take the wise precaution of ordering royal troops to stand by on the alert.

As Viracocha's dream had foreseen, rebellion broke out among the once-loyal Inca province, and only the quick action taken by the royal troops garrisoned nearby was able to keep the northern tribes under the royal command. It had been as Viracocha had perceived in his warning dream, and the momentarily doubtful father would never again question the strange messages of the future that came to his son at night.

On another occasion, the prince dreamed of a strong army of invaders marching toward the Inca capital of Cuzco from the south. The enemy counted on surprise as they moved secretly through the jungle trails, and they planned to attack before the Inca could prepare for war.

Viracocha saw clearly the treacherous route that the invaders had chosen for their surprise attack. The Inca had always counted on the thick and hostile jungle as a part of their capital city's natural defense. Even the young prince found it difficult to believe that this dream could be true.

Although he had come to trust in the accuracy of his son's visions, the king was incredulous when Viracocha repeated the details of his latest warning dream. No enemy had ever been able to penetrate the hostile jungle in the history of the Inca empire. Although it seemed highly unlikely that the present enemy could succeed where other invaders had failed, the king had to consider the veracity of his son's earlier visions.

As before, being above all things a practical and a prudent man, the king ordered the high priests to study the signs revealed in the intestines of a young llama and to divine any omens that might provide substantiation of Viracocha's dream.

As the priests examined the slippery entrails of the sacrificial animal, they grew to become as one mind. The dream of Viracocha had been correct. The omens declared that even now the enemy was making haste to fall upon Cuzco.

The king named his son to lead the royal army in defense of the empire's capital, and Viracocha was able to plot a cunning death trap for the invaders--because he had seen the precise movements of their secret strategy in a dream. Once again the empire of the Inca had been saved, thanks to the precognitive dreams of their prince.

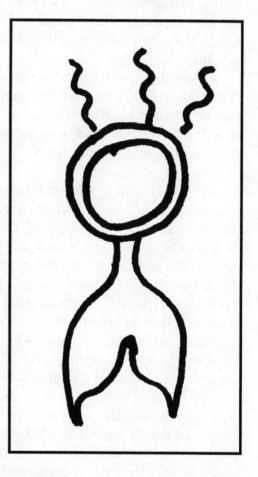

Symbol of Manabozho, a culture bearing figure for the eastern tribes.

The legends of the strangely gifted young prince's ability to divine the future are many, and Viracocha has gained the status of a supernatural being in the folklore of Peru. Indeed, his name was taken from the Inca god to whom they attributed the creation of life, and it truly seemed that he had come from the dimension of the ancient deities and that they maintained an open line of communication with him through his truthtelling dreams.

Viracocha's most troubling dreams had to do with pale-colored men with beards who would come to the land of the Incas from afar. He saw them arrive in great ships, and he watched as they donned armor that danced in the sun and blinded his eyes. The strange, pale men sat astride unfamiliar animals of great size, and in their hands they carried a rod that flashed fire and death for the Inca.

Viracocha spent many hours pondering the meaning of the bizarre dream. Surely, there could be no such men and no such creatures. There were no weapons that killed with flames and the noise of thunder. Why was this dream so different from all the rest of his night visions?

The Inca prince was so taken by his haunting dream that he ordered craftsmen to begin building a great temple, one that consisted of twelve corridors leading to a center temple in which he would fashion with his own hands a likeness of the pale, bearded men who menaced his slumber.

When Viracocha became king, his remarkable ability to dream true enabled him to save his empire from the scheming of a false friend, who was plotting to usurp the throne. In his night vision, Viracocha perceived a cup of wine receiving a draught of poison. Then, to his dismay, he saw a man he had cherished as a friend serving him the deadly mixture. As the dream unfolded its tragic drama, Viracocha drank the poisoned wine and fell dead. In the turmoil that followed his death, Viracocha foresaw an alternate dream reality that showed the conspirators seizing control of the mighty Inca kingdom.

On the evening of the festival for which the assassination was planned, Viracocha made certain that the throne room was filled with some of his most loyal supporters, all secretly armed.

Somewhat unnerved by the number of witnesses, but determined to go ahead with the plot, the assassin stepped forward with the poisoned cup of wine.

"O my king, please let me present a special gift for you on the eve of this most sacred festival," the man began, gathering his courage. "As you are well aware, the tasks you assign me cause me to travel widely, and thusly I am able to experience many sights and pleasures not available to other officials in the empire. Permit me then, to share with you a cup of a wine of most marvelous quality that I discovered in the western provinces. Its bold, yet subtle, blend of fruits make this wine an experience that you shall never forget."

Viracocha accepted the wine from the deceiver with a small nod of approval and anticipation. He raised a hand as if to drink deeply from the goblet, then paused reflectively.

"My friend," he spoke softly to the assassin, "we have raised many a goblet of delightful wine together. As my companion of so many pleasant evenings, please sample the wine and tell me if it is as cool as I like it."

The villain's forehead was suddenly moist with beads of sweat, and he smiled nervously, knowing that all eyes in the throne room were fast upon him.

"I know that the wine is as my lord most enjoys it," he managed to push past the tension that was freezing his tongue.

"Ah, but you have stood there holding it for so long," Viracocha argued, "your hand must certainly have warmed the wine. Drink some, and tell me if it is still cool enough for my taste."

The false friend's hand began to tremble wildly, and the Inca king knew once again that he had dreamed true.

"Why do you not drink the wine and please me?" Viracocha demanded, his eyes suddenly fierce with the full knowledge of his friend's treachery. The king knew that his old companion had never truly believed in the power of prophetic dreams that he possessed. And now, even though Viracocha wished with all his heart that it were not so, the deceitful friend had discovered fully the accuracy of the king's night visions.

Summoning his officers and the loyal members of the Incan aristocracy, Viracocha ordered the assassin executed in his presence--then he left the throne room to weep.

Feminine Moon spirit that brings prophetic powers to devout Medicine Priests.

On another dramatic, yet more pleasant, occasion, Viracocha saved a young woman from death after her image had come to him in a series of dreams to plead for the life of her yet-unborn child. The woman, the dreams told him, was a captive who had been seized in a raid against rebels in the west. She had been marked for death at a forthcoming festival in which human sacrifices were offered to the gods.

During the course of the fifth such dream, the captive woman fell at the hem of the king's royal robe and begged to be allowed to give birth to her child. Viracocha saw clearly the manner in which the young woman bound her long, dark hair in a large top knot.

He also took notice of a gold bracelet on her left wrist which bore the symbol of a serpent entwined about a pole.

"Once the child is born," she pleaded, "you may do with me that which you will. Only let my son be born, for it is his destiny to lead men."

So strong were the urgings in the fifth dream that Viracocha roused himself and went to the place where the new prisoners were kept. He had to see for himself if such a woman as the one who haunted his night visions truly existed.

The officers at the prison said that they had seen no such woman as the king described. Viracocha made ready to leave, puzzled that for the first time his dreams had not revealed a literal truth. Perhaps the gods meant to teach him a lesson through symbols. He would hurry back to his chambers to study the design of the dreams and to learn their true meaning.

As he was leaving through the prison gate, a new band of captives were being roughly ushered inside the walls. As the stream of prisoners moved past him, one young woman dropped from the line of forced march and fell at his feet. Before guards could snatch her back into line, she had clutched the hem of the royal robe and had begun to plead for the life of her unborn son.

It was as it had been in Viracocha's dream; and he beheld the same manner in which she bound her long, dark hair, and he recognized the serpent on her bracelet.

To the astonishment of the guards, the king ordered the woman cut free of her bonds and commanded that she be taken to the royal palace.

After the woman had been made presentable, Viracocha had her brought before him, and he began to question her about the particulars of the series of dreams in which she had appeared so prominently.

Somehow the perceptive young ruler was not surprised when she related that she was the daughter of a king who ruled an eastern kingdom and that she had been married to a prince of royal blood. With great conviction, she went on to state that the child she carried in her womb had been dedicated to the gods at the time of conception.

"He will one day rule over his people and be of great service to the Inca," she said firmly without the slightest tremor of indecision or doubt.

The princess told Viracocha that she, too, had experienced a series of remarkable dreams. "Each night as the harsh, relentless warriors granted us rest along the agonizing march to an Inca prison, I dreamt that I visited a handsome young king as he slept in his bedchamber," she told him. "On each visit, I begged him to spare my life for the sake of my unborn child. When I saw you at the prison gate, my lord, I recognized you as the young king in my dreams."

Viracocha listened with great interest, then took the woman to inspect the royal bedchamber.

"It is the very room in which I walked during my dreams," she verified. "And you are the young king to whom I have pled my case."

Viracocha smiled and nodded his head at her testimony. Once again, he had dreamed true.

Certain that the gods had spoken clearly in the dreams, Viracocha ordered an honor guard to escort the princess back to her own people. He sent gifts with a trusted officer and gave him firm instructions that he was to apologize to the woman's family that her journey had been so thoughtlessly interrupted by Inca soldiers.

And true to the words that the young woman had spoken in Viracocha's dreams and in her visit to the royal chambers, the son whom she bore grew to great power as the ruler of his own kingdom--and in the later years of Viracocha came to the aid of the Inca in a crucial battle they might otherwise have lost.

But of all the dreams that came to Viracocha, none was more persistent and foreboding than the ones which foretold the coming of the pale, bearded men with the strange animals and the deadly thunder sticks. And

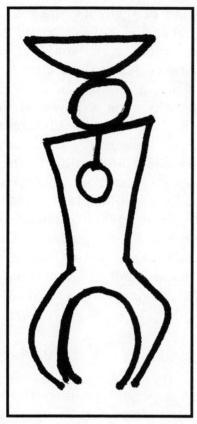

Spirit of the Great Waters.

unthinkable as it seemed, the ruler of the Inca knew
that these bizarre invaders would conquer his people.

Viracocha, the eighth king of the Inca empire, did
not live to see the accuracy of the most frightening of
his precognitive dreams. The pale-faced men with beards
would come in great ships, and they would enslave the
Inca with the might of fire rods that spoke with the
voice of thunder and shattered the bodies of the stron-
gest warriors.

The pale ones would come during the reign of the
twelfth and final ruler of the Inca, and they would
walk with sturdy conquerors' boots through the temple
of twelve corridors that Viracocha had built. They
were the Spanish *conquistadors*, and they looked exactly
like the statue that young prince Viracocha had carved
to match the men in his dreams.

If you have become aware of thoughts, images, and inspirations from a source that you believe to be the spirit energy of the great Viracocha, it would behoove you to undergo a brief period of fasting and a process of serious self-evaluation and self-discipline in order to determine the exact reason why such a powerful vibration has made contact with you. You should carefully analyze the messages that you have received for any Medicine symbols that may add clarification to the communications which you have received. Once you feel certain that you have established solid clues to the reason for the contact, prepare to enter the silence of deep meditation to seek more complete guidance. Quite likely, your Higher Self is being activated to fulfill your true mission on this planet, and you are being alerted to be of meaningful service to the Earth Mother and all of her children.

White Cloud

Chief White Cloud was a great mystic-warrior of the Winnebago, whose dreams from the Great Mystery seemed always to foretell the future. He knew that things would be no different on that night when he sat studying the small dancing flames that rose and fell in the fire pit before his lodge.

It was nearly dawn when he summoned the council of elders to hear the words of his vision. "We will leave this place soon," White Cloud said, referring to the Winnebago's small village on the Rock River in what the white man called the Illinois Territory. "The white ones will come soon and drive us away. Our brothers from the Sac and the Fox will stream through our villages, seeking refuge. Our villages will be destroyed."

The seer's words were met with angered cries of outrage from those who encircled him. This time White Cloud had to be wrong. Even now the great war chief Black Hawk of the Sac and Fox tribes was setting out

to punish the white evildoers and to regain Indian land.
But within each chest beat a sinking, painful heart.
They knew that White Cloud's words from the Great
Mystery always left great footprints of truth in the
sand of time. It was the accuracy of his visions that had
earned him the name of "the Prophet" among the
Winnebago.

The Winnebago were among a number of tribes
which the advancing white settlers had harried in their
endless quest to claim the rich prairies as their own.
While the Winnebago watched the white invader carefully and saw their hunting grounds transformed into
corn and wheat fields, they remained peaceful.

Symbol of
bad weather
and
misfor-
tune.

It was for the great Black Hawk to lead revengeful
strikes against the settlers. The Winnebago knew that
Black Hawk had been patient time after time and had
closed his eyes to terrible acts of violence and thievery
on the part of the whites. Now, at last, in the spring
of 1832, he was lashing out at those who would violate
the Earth Mother and her peaceful children.

"Black Hawk will make the bad whites pay for
what they have done to the Indian people," members of

the Winnebago council told White Cloud. "This time
your vision was not true. Black Hawk will push the
white man back into the oceans."

Black Hawk began his war with a series of daring
raids, but soon he was forced to retreat as strategically
as possible with a pursuing army of militia on his
heels.

The war had begun in the month the whites called
"April." In early May, battered remnants of Black
Hawk's raiding parties were streaming through
Winnebago villages in flight from a heavily armed
militia. Among those soldiers in pursuit of the fleeing
Sac and Fox was a young volunteer from Salem, Illinois,
named Abraham Lincoln, who would later speak of his
regret for much of what had been done to the Indian
tribes that had been victimized by the white man's rush
to claim the prairie for seed and cities.

On the night of May 10, 1832, White Cloud once
more summoned the elders to him and reminded them of
his vision. "You have now seen the events of my dream.
You have seen our Sac and Fox brothers running for
their lives through our villages. Soon the white army
will destroy our own villages and drive us from our
land."

The militia arrived in White Cloud's village on the
very next day. Although the elders stated firmly that
the Winnebago had not joined Black Hawk's war, the
officers stated that the village was to be burned.

"No, that is not just," Standing Bear, the oldest
member of the council spoke out, rising feebly to confront a lieutenant with a waxed handlebar mustache.
"We have given no aid to Black Hawk. We did not
support his raids. We have raised no hand against the
white man."

Standing Bear's protest was not considered eligible
for discussion or deliberation. The Winnebago village
was put to the torch and burned to the ground by an
angry, shouting, menacing white militia.

It had been as White Cloud had foreseen. The glowing coals of his campfire had foreshown him the dying

ashes of his own peaceful village.

Sadly, the remainder of White Cloud's tragic dream would also come to pass: The Winnebago would be driven from their lands.

The Black Hawk war was over in September, five months after it had begun. Once the treaty had been signed, the lush prairie where the Winnebago had made their home for generations was opened to the endless march of the white men, who came with wagons, homesteads, and iron plows to turn over the grass where the buffalo had fed. Soon, the Winnebago had been pushed back, White Cloud with them, and his grim prophecy had been fulfilled.

To the Winnebago it had been a bitter glimpse of the future, but to the white settlers White Cloud's remarkable talents of precognition were honored when it came

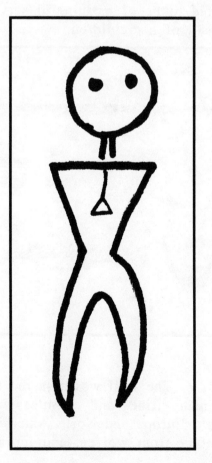

Symbol of one
with an open heart,
a spiritual seeker.

time to name the town that rose from the ashes of his village. To this day, Prophetstown, Illinois, stands as memorial to the mystic Winnebago chief who heard the Great Mystery speak in his dreams and his visions. Perhaps it was best that the most tragic dream was saved for the last.

If you have become convinced that you have been receiving thoughts, images, and inspirations from a source that you believe to be the spirit energy of the great White Cloud, you should undergo a process of self-evaluation and self-discipline in order to determine the exact reason why such a powerful vibration has made contact with you. Once you feel certain that you have established solid clues to the motive for the contact, prepare to enter the silence of deep meditation to seek more complete guidance. Quite likely, you are being alerted to be of meaningful service to the Earth Mother and all of her children.

Zuni wolf fetish.

WOLF The wolf was a sacred totem and a clan symbol for many tribes and countless individuals throughout all of old Europe and North America. Many heroes claimed ancestry from wolves, and lupine mothers figure prominently in the birth and/or the nurturing of legendary, archetypal beings, such as Romulus and Remus, the founders of Rome.

Idealization of the wolf's prowess, endurance, and cunning led both to its worship and to the adoption of its persona. Such strong and intense identification blended quite naturally to form tales of werewolves, those humans who possessed the power to become wolves.

Grandmother Twylah, a spokesperson for the Wolf Clan of the Seneca, has observed that from the wolf the Indian learned forethought before decision, the importance of family loyalty and unity, and the knowledge of a great deal of his Medicine Power.

If your dreams, visions, and personal quest have revealed the wolf as your totem animal, then its manifestation in any of your dreams will have been designed by your guide to alert you to the subsequent display of a series of important symbols that will be certain to follow the appearance of the wolf. These symbols, once carefully analyzed, will provide essential clues that will aid you in solving any problems that may be vexing you.

If your dream scenario depicted you in a scene where you were frightened by the appearance of a wolf, you must be on guard against a robbery or a burglary.

A dream in which your guide portrayed you as walking through a forest and seeing a wolf running ahead of you provided you with a symbol that prosperity and better times are just ahead of you. If the wolf suddenly ran past you, then you are being warned that very clever enemies could delay the arrival of your good fortune.

If you dreamed that you were being followed by a number of wolves, you should be alerted to the possibility that some people very close to you are taking advantage of your trust. If two or more of the pursuing wolves should begin playing together and ignoring you, you must also be aware of false friends who are conspiring to deceive you.

Brother Wolf.

A dream scenario which depicts you running after a wolf and catching it has offered you a symbol of an abundance of money that will soon come into your grasp. If you tamed the wolf after capturing it, you are being warned that your love relationship could be damaged by your mishandling of the money you are about to receive. If you killed the wolf after you caught it, you could soon lose the recently acquired money if you do not plan carefully for its wise dispersal.

Wovoka

For the white man, the last decade of the previous century was called the Gay Nineties. For the red man, it was the decade that marked the death of the old ways, the entombment of the Great Spirit, and a surrender to an alien culture. Then came Wovoka, the Paiute Messiah, the great dreamer who promised his people a shining path to a rebirth of spirit and a new age of peace.

A strange fire burned within the heart of Wovoka, who was called Jack Wilson by the white men. He was powerfully built, darkly handsome, and just under six feet tall. His grandfather was the esteemed prophet Wodziwob. His father was the holy man Tavibo. By his own people, Wovoka was also called "the Cutter." To some, those who knew that he listened to voices in the wind, he was One with the Morning Star on His Head.

Then came the day during an eclipse of the sun when a terrible fever entered Wovoka's body, and for three days he lay in death. His wife, Mary, had permitted those closest to him to test his flesh with fire and knife. He was dead. He had fallen when the Sky Monster ate the sun. His friends fired their guns at the Sky Monster to make it spit out the sun; and, at last, it became light again. The sun lived, but Wovoka did not. He lay stretched out on furs and hides.

When Wovoka returned to life and to the arms of his wife, he told those assembled around him of the vision

that he had received. He had walked in the Other World
with the Old Man. He had been told that the Earth
Mother, just as the sun, just as Wovoka himself, would
die. Thunders would come. The Earth Mother would
begin to shake. Smoke would come out of the ground.
Lightning would crash all around. Indians should go to
the high country to await the Earth Mother's death in
safety--but no Indian should be afraid, for the earth
would come alive again, just as the sun, just as Wovoka
had come alive again.

The spirit captain that some people called God told
Wovoka that the grandmothers and grandfathers in the
Other World were all alive, waiting to be reborn in the
New World. All Indians and good whites would be
reborn without disease or pain. All those who did not
believe--white and red--would be swept off the face of
the earth.

If the Indians wished the buffalo to return, the
grasses to grow tall, the rivers to run clean, they must
not injure anyone; they must not do harm to any living
thing. They must not hate the white man. They must
not make war. They must lead lives of purity. They
must cease gambling, put away strong drink, and never
again sell the bodies of their wives to satisfy the lusts
of the white man.

The most important part of the vision that the Great
Spirit gave to Wovoka was the Ghost Dance. To help
the New World be born, the Indian people must perform a special dance that the Old Man said had never
been performed anywhere on Earth. It was the dance of
the spirit people of the Other World. The performance
of this dance would insure that God's blessings would
be bestowed upon the tribes. To follow the movements
of this dance would make the Indian free once more. It
would bring back the buffalo and the tall grasses.

Wovoka said that the Great Spirit had spoken to him
as though he were his son, the same way that God the
Father had talked with Jesus of Nazareth. The Old Man
had told Wovoka that many miracles would be worked

through him. In his heart and in his life path, Wovoka became Jesus; Mason Valley, Nevada, became Galilee; and the American Indians had received their own messiah.

It took only days for the words of the new Indian prophet to blaze their way across mountains, prairies, and deserts and to burn deeply into the hearts of those who heard the message of what must be done to save the Indian nations from extinction. Soon the greatest Medicine priests from all the tribes were gathering to hear the words of Wovoka, the words that had been revealed to him by the Great Mystery.

"We must dance," Wovoka told his enraptured listeners. "We must dance the dance of ghosts and then all of those grandmothers and grandfathers who have gone before us will return. And there will be thousands and tens of thousands and ten times more. The Indian people will be reborn on the Earth Mother."

By the hundreds they danced and chanted, their feet touching the earth in ceremonial rapture. They called upon the ghosts of the old chiefs to come to join them. They sang to the buffalo to raise their rotting bones from the prairie. They prayed to the spirits to fill their hearts with renewed hope.

Soon men and women from many tribes saw the truth of Wovoka's vision of peace, and they began to call him Jesus. His fame spread so far and wide that newspaper reporters came from St. Louis, New York, and Chicago to see the Ghost Dance Messiah and to record his words.

But many warriors listened to the words of Wovoka and felt their hearts sink even deeper into despair. They had hoped for a strong holy man with powerful Medicine to drive the white man from their lands, but Wovoka spoke only of the importance of all men living together in harmony--and he shook off all the importuning hands that begged him to use his powers to drive the evil ones from the nation.

Sitting Bull, the great Sioux prophet, listened carefully to Wovoka's vision of a return to glory for all

Indian people. Within the Sioux people, a visionary perceived that rather than wearing the long gowns of Wovoka's disciples, a specially decorated Ghost Shirt could turn the bullets of the white soldiers to water. Such medicine could transform the Sioux into invincible warriors. Sitting Bull decreed that only by purging the white men from the land would the grasses once again grow tall...only by driving the white men to the sea could the buffalo return...only by removing the white men and their factories could the rivers once more run clean.

Symbol of the Great
Mystery as Creator of the
Universe.

The Sioux began to dance wearing their Ghost Shirts, and soon newspapers in the Dakotas were warning nervous and fearful settlers that the red men were preparing for war. When the warriors at Sitting Bull's Grand River camp began to dance with rifles, the white soldiers agreed that a great Indian revolt was about to occur. Even the sympathetic journalists and military officers could now see that the dance of peace and love was really a war dance of hate and revenge.

Inflamed by the passions of the Ghost Dance, Sitting Bull vowed that the Sioux at Standing Rock Agency would fight to the death to drive the white man away. Now that the Great Spirit had made known his plan to help the Indians bring back the buffalo and sweep the white men into the sea, the Sioux would lead the first charge.

On December 14, 1890, Indian police, Fouchet's Cavalry, and Drum's Infantry moved against the Sioux camp at Grand River. The aggressors also brought with them Hotchkiss multiple-firing guns and mountain howitzers. One of the first shots killed Sitting Bull. The soldiers, the automatic rifles, the exploding shells destroyed the village.

When Wovoka learned of the horror, he went into retreat in his cabin in Mason Valley, guarded by loyal Paiutes who feared military reprisals against their messiah.

Wovoka did not understand why the Sioux had performed the Ghost Dance incorrectly. He did not know where they had received the vision of the buckskin and cotton shirts with the fringes and the wrong pictures painted on them. He could not comprehend why Sitting Bull had declared himself high priest of the Ghost Dancers. Some bad spirit had told Sitting Bull a false and terrible thing.

Wovoka had only begun to recover from the shattering news of Sitting Bull's fate when word reached him of the dawn attack on Big Foot's camp at Wounded Knee on December 29. As they were being slaughtered by two battalions of soldiers, the Sioux had sung Ghost Dance songs, blended with their own death chants, and had thrown dust into the air as a symbol of the coming storm that would bury the white men.

Wovoka knew in his heart that he had only told others what the Great Spirit had told him. He had taught the movements of the dance carefully and in complete fidelity to the instructions of God. He wept bitterly because his teachings had been distorted.

The massacre at Wounded Knee snuffed the last sparks of hope that the fiery words of the Paiute messiah had set ablaze in the hearts of the red men. All men knew now that words, no matter how impassioned and true, could not bring back the great warriors, the mighty chiefs, and the sacred Medicine priests that the white men's guns and diseases had taken. No amount of dancing would transform old people into virile young men and women. No amount of chanting would allow the spirits of the dead to return to the world of the living. Nor would the slaughtered buffalo resume their lordship of the plains. Nor would the day ever dawn again when a horseman could ride for a dozen tomorrows and hear no voice on the prairie other than the Great Spirit's.

In early October of 1932, the white spirit horse stopped at Wovoka's door. The old one knew that the Great Mystery had sent for him, and he went willingly to the land of plentiful game, tall grasses, and loving spirits that he had visited so many years ago.

On the night Wovoka died, a number of still-faithful disciples took the sound of his dying breath as a signal to perform the Ghost Dance once again. Many of the dancers that night swore that the spirit of the Paiute messiah joined the circle and danced a final turn to the solemn beat of ancient drums.

If you have become convinced that you have been receiving thoughts, images, and inspirations from a source that you believe to be the spirit energy of the great Wovoka, it would behoove you to undergo a brief period of fasting and a process of serious self-evaluation and self-discipline in order to determine the exact reason why such a powerful vibration has made contact with you. You should carefully analyze the messages that you have received for any Medicine symbols that may add clarification to the communications which you have received. Once you feel certain that you have established solid clues to the reason for the contact, prepare to enter the silence of deep meditation to seek more complete guidance. Quite likely, your Higher Self is being activated to fulfill your true mission on this planet, and you are being alerted to be of meaningful service to the Earth Mother and all of her children.

Traveling To and Fro in Dreamtime

My friend Gray Owl once explained what traveling in Dreamtime was like for him: "When I see my totem, the great white owl, I know that I am ready to leave my body and travel in Dreamtime. In my dream, I visualize myself rocking back in forth in my physical body. Pretty soon I hear a kind of snapping noise, and my spirit seems to roll away from all the rest of my body and move toward my head. Next, I just move out of my skull."

Gray Owl said that he first appears looking something like a jellyfish or a large egg yolk. "I kind of bob up and down," he continued, "and then I expand to my full stature-- although I am kind of translucent, bluish in color...and completely naked. Then, because I don't know for certain where I'll go traveling and if, by chance, I might be seen, I will myself to cover my bare body and to be clothed.

"I never see things on the earth plane that are as clear, distinct, and colorful as they exist in Dreamtime. I am able to soar high into the sky and look down at the world below me. If I have to go through a ceiling or a wall, it feels kind of like moving through suspended feathers. It kind of tickles.

"Many times on my travels in Dreamtime I see a friend or a loved one who is now in the spirit world.

Sometimes we speak; other times, we do not," Gray Owl said. "On occasion, I have encountered some entity that is evil and threatening. I always call upon the white owl, my guide, to come near me and to send me spiritual help.

"Sometimes people see me in my spirit body," he laughed. "Sometimes I give people a good scare.

"Not long ago, I traveled to the bedroom of a woman I like very much. I was just hovering above her, watching her; and all of a sudden, she woke up and saw me. Her eyes opened very wide, and she gave out a little scream. I got out of there fast. The next day, though, she called me and asked just what I thought I was up to."

Gray Owl said that he had learned to travel in Dreamtime simply by repeated utterance of the following affirmation:

>"Great Mystery, I am now lying down to sleep in the comfort of the awareness that all life is good and all life is one. Tonight I ask that my Dreamtime be meaningful and filled with wisdom and knowledge. During my Dreamtime, may my totem guide attend my spirit self, keep me secure from all bad spirits, and grant me a safe return to my physical body."

If a particular target was sought by Gray Owl, as in the case of his vivid "Peeping Tom" incident with his lady friend, he would simply add:

"During my Dreamtime I wish to travel to visit _____. I will do this person no harm or violate his (her) individual sovereignty in any way. I know that I have the ability to travel safe through time and space and to be in the presence of _____ instantly."

Gray Owl stressed that he never forgot the part of the affirmation that asked his guide for protection from all bad spirits. Such cautions must always be exercised.

Another Medicine friend, Starwolf, said that her technique of traveling to and fro in Dreamtime involved a photograph of the person whom she wished to visit that night and the writing of his or her name on a piece of paper.

"I simply lie quietly in my bed, looking at the photograph and thinking of my friend for an indeterminate period of time," Starwolf said. "Then I write my friend's name on a notepad and place my finger on his or her name. Again, the period of time during which I keep my finger on the name is indeterminate. It might be a few seconds or a few minutes.

"Then I shut off the lights, settle back to sleep, and float into the farthest reaches of Dreamtime. In no time at all, or so it seems, I am with the person whom I 'targeted' for that night."

Sometimes people travel in Dreamtime to places that they have yet to visit in their physical bodies. Alice Windwalker said that one day she lay down to take a short nap after lunch and suddenly found herself traveling in Dreamtime.

Suddenly she was in a hotel room. "It was a place that I had never been," Alice stated, "but at first I thought that it was not unlike other motel or hotel rooms that I had visited at one time or another in my life. I took note of the furniture, the bedspread, the rules for overnight guests tacked behind the door.

"When I entered the bathroom, I was surprised to see that the tub had these old-fashioned claw legs, the kind that curve out and appear to be clutching the metal balls that rest on the floor. Although the rest of the room seemed very modern and up-to-date, the bathroom seemed to be striving for some kind of quaint, back-in-time look.

"Leaving the bathroom, I looked out the window in the bedroom and saw a neon sign flashing off and on and advertising dairy products from Sutter's Farm.

"I was about to leave the room and to do some more Dreamtime exploring of whatever place I was visiting, when I felt myself being pulled back to my body and to wakefulness. There was a rapid rush of images, and I was back on my couch, looking into the laughing faces of my husband and two sons. They teased me about being such a sound sleeper and forgetting about the movie we were going to see that afternoon. They said that they had been trying to awaken me for several minutes.

"About a month or so later," Alice said, "my sister was involved in an automobile accident in Prairie du Chien, Wisconsin, and I went to visit her in the hospital. Since she had recently been divorced and had no one else to be with her, I told her that I would stay for another two or three days until she felt a little better.

"A nurse recommended a hotel, and somehow I was not surprised to check in and to discover the room of my afternoon nap Dreamtime visit. The bathtub had those old-fashioned claw legs, and the neon sign flashing outside the window advertised Sutter's Farm dairy products."

Alice concluded her account by stating that she is convinced that if her husband and sons had not awakened when they did, she would have stayed in Dreamtime long enough to receive a forewarning from her guide about her sister's accident.

Micah Beartooth, a Chippewa from northern Minnesota, who is becoming a very accomplished Medicine practitioner, remembers how he first began traveling in Dreamtime when he was a teenager working for Norwegian-American farmers in the area.

"Maybe we'd be putting up hay, and I'd sneak a little nap after the noon meal. I'd crawl up on some hay bales, close my eyes, and I would travel in Dreamtime for a while. Usually, I would just check and see what my friends--and especially my girl friend--were doing."

It wasn't long before his spirit guides were coming to travel with Micah in Dreamtime. "I was probably fifteen or so when my guides started coming for me when I would lie down to sleep at night. Some times they would appear like majestic, glowing beings--a tall, strong chief and a beautiful woman in white deerskin. Other times, they would manifest as a bear and a deer, but I knew they were the same spirit entities. They would travel with me in Dreamtime to an awesome council fire where I could see the forms of many spirit beings sitting around the flames with their blankets up around their faces. It was at this council fire in Dreamtime that my guides taught me about the old ways, the old traditions, and how to practice Medicine Power on my earthwalk."

How To Protect Yourself from Negative Entities In Dreamtime

When Robert Segee set the fire on that summer day in Hartford, Connecticut, he was obeying the command of a fiery Indian warrior who sat astride a blazing stallion and told him that he must punish the white man for the wrongs done to the American Indian. On that particular day in the summer of 1944, Segee punished 169 white men and women--and many of their children, too. Tragically, his match ignited the canvas of the big top at the Ringling Brothers Circus.

When at last the twenty-one year-old Ohioan was confined for treatment of mental illness in 1950, the tragic saga of Indian revenge from beyond the grave was revealed to the shocked and disbelieving ears of psychiatrists and police authorities. Segee told of setting dozens of fires in a pyromaniacal path that spread from the northeast coast to the plains states.

Always, the young man said, he was told that he must be the instrument of Indian revenge. Always, he was driven to his incendiary acts by the vision of the fiery Indian brave. The flaming horseman commanded the young half-breed to burn again and again, until the red men were avenged. The apparition told him when to strike and when to flee to avoid capture.

Readers of *Life* magazine saw crude, red-crayon sketches that Segee had drawn while in confinement that depicted the flaming horse and rider who ordered him to set the fires that charred innocent victims.

During his trial on murder charges in connection with the deaths of four persons whose lives had been snuffed out by his arson, Segee was declared insane by psychiatrists who examined him. We would expect such a decree from the disciples of psychological orthodoxy.

As students of metaphysics and Medicine, however, we may consider that Segee's burning mission of terror was guided by vengeful spirits from the Other World-- the angry mental forces of those Indians who had long ago suffered cruelty, death, and virtual annihilation at the hands of whites who had first violated, then claimed, their sacred lands. Indeed, Robert Segee may well have been possessed by such spirits and rendered powerless to do anything other than obey the deadly commands to burn and to kill.

Once when I was discussing such cases as that of the tragic Robert Segee, Samuel Little Turtle, a very wise Medicine Priest, told me that there is always a great danger of spirit possession for the neophyte Medicine practitioner who does not observe the proper practices of asking for protection from the guide. "You must understand," Little Turtle said, "there are numerous spirits who may be earthbound and still desirous of inhabiting a physical body. Some feel that they have left too many tasks undone, and they wish another body and another chance to complete their labors on the Earth Mother.

"In the case of Indian spirits, it is, as Chief Seattle said, the 'invisible dead of many tribes' who will haunt this land for ever. There are those who lie in unmarked graves, their bones scattered by scavengers, victims of dawn massacres when soldiers attacked peaceful vil- lages. There are those who lie in mass graves, victims of smallpox, measles, and other white man's diseases.

"Although these restless spirits may cry out for revenge and may take possession of the living to accom- plish vengeance, they are basically good entities, the victims of injustice, who can be reached by Medicine Power and who can be helped to adjust to life on the spiritual planes. Most of these spirits are caught in a nowhere place, just short of the spirit world of the grandparents. A skillful Medicine Priest can help them forget about revenge and assist them to cross over to the heart of the Great Mystery.

"But it is the evil entities that one must really be on guard against in Dreamtime," Little Turtle emphasized. "These wretched creatures of darkness are always seeking a passive, living body to invade. That is why a wise practitioner of Medicine or one who wishes to travel in Dreamtime will always lie down to sleep in an attitude of reverence. To guard against such bad spirits, you should always say a prayer and ask for your guide to protect you while you travel in Dreamtime."

Another of my talented Medicine friends, John LaDue, who regularly travels in Dreamtime, told me of frightening encounter that he had experienced one night when he had decided to journey to visit his parents' home.

"As I lay down to sleep," John began his account, "I concentrated for several minutes on my parents' photographs. They're getting up in years now, and I like to look in on them from time to time to be certain that they are both well. If I simply called them on the telephone, they would tell me they were fine even if they were seriously ill. When I visit them in Dreamtime, I can be certain of knowing how they really are."

Continuing his eerie tale, John said that he had scarcely arrived at the familiar surroundings of his parents' home when he seemed to sense an aura of malignant evil. He began to feel a strange vibration that he had never before experienced in Dreamtime.

"Looking behind me, I was horrified to see a shapeless black mass that seemed to be swirling toward me. In a flash of insight, I understood that this disgusting black mass wished somehow to conquer my spirit so that it could take over my physical body! I was filled with a sense of loathing when I considered that such a thing of evil might usurp my fleshly shell. I knew that I had to return to my body and wake up at once.

"Somehow, most likely telepathically, the thing told me that there was no use in my struggling. It had come to take control of my body. It was stronger than I, so why should I resist it?

"I resolved not to be intimidated by it," John said. "Summoning all my will power, I dove right through it--and although I was momentarily stunned and shocked by its energy, I was not stopped by it.

"Then the race began. The evil entity seemed to be pacing me, side by side, as I raced back in Dreamtime to my physical body. In an instant, I was back in my bedroom, but I was terror-stricken to see that the spirit being had enveloped my body in a black cloud.

"Each time I would attempt to enter my body," John recalled, "I would be rebuffed and be sent bouncing back into Dreamtime. I cried out to my guide for help, and it appeared in the totem form of the eagle. It circled the evil spirit, flapping its huge, powerful wings, and jabbing at it with its great beak. Although the black cloud withdrew slightly from my physical body, it by no means retreated from the onslaughts of my guide.

"Then I heard my guide's voice reverberating within my very essence: 'You have the ability to save yourself. You have within your spirit the power to conquer evil.'

"Reassured, I exercised the full force of my will and pressed into the black cloud enveloping my physical body," John continued. "I seemed to be surrounded by an inky blackness. I felt as if I were falling through space...like a meteorite hitting the atmosphere, being turned into flaming dust by friction.

"In the next instant, I was opening my eyes, only dimly aware of my body on my bed," John said. "I gave thanks to God, the Great Mystery, my guide, and to the heart of love in the universe for guiding me back to my body. I felt weak and nauseated. But I had learned a valuable lesson: I will never again lie down to enter and to travel in Dreamtime without a prayer to the Great Mystery to protect me and a request to my guide to accompany me and watch over me."

Some years ago when I was conducting regular experiments in mind travel during Dreamtime, a young woman named Carol decided to put her lessons into action. She went to bed early and put on the cassette tape that she had made in my workshop that afternoon. In essence, the tape placed the subject into a deep state of relaxation, then led her or him into a controlled out-of-body projection.

"I decided that I would concentrate on the house of a nearby neighbor, so that I would be able to verify the surroundings with a visit in the next day or so," she said later, as she recounted the frightening experience of that night. "I found that I could accomplish the travel quite readily, but I had difficulty controlling it. I knew that I had arrived in my neighbors' living room, so I started to look around for them. When I couldn't see them on the main floor, I began to climb the stairs in search of them."

It was as she was climbing the stairs that the area around her became darker. Carol knew that she was losing control of her spirit body in Dreamtime. She described a sensation of something holding her back. "I seemed rooted in one spot," she said, "and I was beginning to feel very threatened.

It was at this point that Carol saw a dark cloud or vapor approaching her. "Somehow I felt that whatever it was, it meant to envelope me," she said. "I had the terrible feeling that it intended to block me from returning to my physical body. As it came closer to me, it assumed a basic human shape, appearing as a tall man in a cape. Although I could not at first distinguish any facial characteristics, I soon perceived two red, glowing eyes under heavy lids and bushy brows. Brownish-yellow wrinkled skin covered a skull that was devoid of all hair other than the thick eyebrows."

Carol knew that she must somehow return to her body, but she could feel the negative power of the entity sapping her energy and her will. "It seemed to be promising me a marvelous existence in this bizarre in-between world," she stated. "It came so close to me that I could count every wrinkle on its loathsome forehead."

At last, with an effort that summoned every bit of her soul strength, Carol visualized her totem guide, the wolf, coming to her rescue, driving back the negative presence. "It seemed as if the very appearance of my totem animal struck the thing like a high-powered spiritual bullet," Carol recalled. "It still took a lot of effort on my part to return to my body and my bed, but it seemed as though my wolf guide walked just a few steps ahead of me, leading me back to safety. When I came back to full wakefulness several hours later, it still seemed as if that monster's awful red eyes were glaring at me. I will never again attempt such an ex-periment without first asking my guide for protection."

After Carol had related her harrowing experience, I explained the techniques of the Golden Medicine Ax of Protection in the event that such a frightening occur-rence should ever again beset her.

"Visualize that you have in your hand a sturdy toma-hawk or ax that has been coated with gleaming gold. See Medicine symbols and the sign of your totem animal etched on its shaft. See colorful bird feathers attached to its shaft. Know that this is your Golden Medicine Ax of Protection and that it has the power to keep evil, negative entities away from you while you travel in Dreamtime--or at any other time when you may feel threatened by the dark side of the force.

"Hold the Golden Medicine Ax of Protection at arm's length and begin to draw a circle around yourself with a tip of the ax's blade. As you turn slowly with the ax at arm's length, you see that a line of gold remains suspended. As you continue to turn with the ax at arm's length, you see that you are creating a golden circle of protection around your physical body.

"When you have completed an entire circle of golden light around your body, see that sparkling stars of energy begin to fall from the circle and form a curtain of living light energy all around you. Hold this image in your mind. Know that nothing evil or negative can penetrate the circle of living light that you have created around your body. Know and understand that nothing can harm you. Know and understand that nothing can enter your golden circle of living light. Know and understand that you can maintain the security of the golden circle of protection as long as you deem it necessary to do so."

Explore the
Universe in
Your Dreamtime

Generally speaking, there seem to be two types of environment for travelling in Dreamtime: 1.) the environment of the earth plane, in which the dream traveler may observe the actions of people and see actual occurrences in faraway places which he or she can later substantiate; and 2.) the geography of other planes of existence, other dimensions of reality, in which the dream traveler may encounter angels, masters, guides, or the spirits of loved ones who have passed away from the physical world.

The ability to travel in Dreamtime is inherent within everyone, and each person's subconscious mind is linked to, and may be attuned with, a Universal Mind. This Universal Mind knows no boundaries of Time and Space and is in harmony with all of the knowledge of both the physical and nonphysical dimensions.

Most people who have had spontaneous psychic experiences--such as telepathic transfer, prophetic glimpses of the future, or mind traveling in Dreamtime--have had them only once or twice in a lifetime. These most likely occurred at completely unexpected moments, and those who had the experiences had absolutely no control over the phenomena.

The practitioners of Medicine Power feel that we would not have been given such abilities unless they were intended to be used in a regular, productive, rewarding manner.

In our Western civilization it has been the accepted thing to seek progress in the fields of science, engineering, and the technologies that bring us our creature comforts. At the same time, the exploration of our inner selves, our souls, has been largely ignored as impractical--or loudly condemned as heretical.

Tragically, the great masses of people in our contemporary society pursue the troubled task of daily survival in their normal, harried conscious state; and they do not take the time to develop the ability to see beyond themselves. On occasion, certain people have flashes of precognition or clairvoyance; but the majority of them journey through their earthwalk perceiving only a very narrow path before them.

However, we live in a marvelous universe of divinely structured order, and the Medicine Priests believe that there is a force within the fabric of our reality that influences all lives and controls all natural laws. It is this force, within and without our individual selves, that is called The Great Mystery, the Wakan, the Ki, the Chi, the Holy Spirit.

On the spiritual level the mind of even the most ardent materialist is ever alert and functioning above all physical boundaries. As it turns out, we, as mortals, have only one true asset--our soul and its linkup with the Great Mystery. The utilization of Dreamtime can make the universe accessible to the common man and woman, to everyone. It is my ardent hope that you will utilize this sourcebook as a guide to future happiness on your earthwalk and as a roadmap to the stars.

I have adapted a very old Indian prayer as an appropriate closing to our study of American Indian dream symbols. Although attribution has been clouded by the years, it is quite likely Delaware or Iroquois in origin:

"Great Mystery, Master of our lives, Master of things visible and invisible, Master of every spirit, good or bad, command the good spirits to be favorable to us and keep the bad spirits from working evil upon us.

"O Grand Mystery, preserve the lives of such of our elders who are inclined to give counsel to the young. Preserve our children and multiply their number and let them be the comfort and support of our declining years. Preserve our corn and our animals, and let no famine desolate our land. Protect our villages and guard our lives.

"Great Mystery, if it now be time for some of us to close our lives on the Earth Mother, let us journey to the great country of spirits where we may meet our friends and loved ones and where you are pleased to shine upon all with a bright, warm, eternal blaze.

"Great Mystery, make known to us your pleasure by sending us the Spirit of Dreams. Let the Spirit of Dreams proclaim thy will in the night, and we will perform it in the day.

"O Grand, O Great Mystery, hearken to our voice. Remember us always, for we are all thy children, descended from thee."